EXCEPTIONAL
YOU!

EXCEPTIONAL YOU!

7 WAYS TO LIVE ENCOURAGED, EMPOWERED, AND INTENTIONAL

VICTORIA OSTEEN

NEW YORK NASHVILLE

FaithWords
Hachette Book Group
1290 Avenue of the Americas, New York, NY 10104
faithwords.com
twitter.com/faithwords

Originally published in hardcover and ebook by FaithWords in April 2019
First Trade Paperback Edition: March 2020

FaithWords is a division of Hachette Book Group, Inc. The FaithWords name and logo are trademarks of Hachette Book Group, Inc.

The publisher is not responsible for websites (or their content) that are not owned by the publisher.

The Hachette Speakers Bureau provides a wide range of authors for speaking events. To find out more, go to www.hachettespeakersbureau.com or call (866) 376-6591.

Library of Congress Control Number: 2018964889

ISBN: 978-1-5460-1062-3 (hardcover), 978-1-5460-3909-9 (signed edition), 978-1-5460-3573-2 (large print), 978-1-5460-1061-6 (ebook), 978-1-5460-1063-0 (trade paperback)

Printed in the United States of America

LSC-C

10 9 8 7 6 5 4 3 2 1

This book is dedicated to my family, whose love enriches my life, and to my Lord and Savior, Whose love enriches my soul

CONTENTS

SECTION V
Love Well

SECTION VI
Live in the Now

SECTION VII
Power Up

INTRODUCTION

When something is exceptional, it means that it is better than good; it is outstanding. The exceptional stands out from the crowd, is extraordinary, and is something to be celebrated. You were made by God to be exceptional.

Scripture says that you are God's masterpiece, formed in His image, and created to do great things. You were wonderfully made, with a purpose and a destiny that is distinctly yours. You didn't come off an assembly line. You're an original. God knew you before you were born and He designed you to be you, unique and exceptional.

But too often we lose sight of who God made us to be. We don't recognize the individual gifts and talents that God has placed in us. If we're not careful, we'll allow our God-given attributes to be reduced in our own minds, causing us to see ourselves as merely average, mediocre, or mundane.

We must understand that God doesn't want us to be ordinary in our thinking or in the way we live our lives. He wants us to be exceptional in every way. God wants us to expect more from ourselves and from Him. He wants us to strive for more and to be the very best that He created us to be.

Every day is a new day with God. His mercies are fresh every morning, regardless of where you find yourself or the difficulties you may be going through. God is by your side. He is always offering us a new beginning and a fresh start.

When I think about the challenges and difficulties I've faced in my life, there were times when I would become discouraged and ask myself, *Is this worth it? Does it even matter?* But today I've realized that when I press through the challenges with faith, I discover the exceptional qualities that God placed in me, and I learn valuable lessons in my life.

We all face challenges and unfair situations, but if we are willing to take steps of faith and place them in God's hands, that's when the exceptional in us is produced.

I've noticed that when I put certain practices in place and incorporate them into my life, I feel myself stepping into my exceptional self each and every day. I've written this book to show you the seven practices that keep me reaching toward the exceptional. They are applications that can keep you encouraged, empowered, and inspired along the way. My hope is that you would read them and put them to use in your life.

God has each of us on a path. No two are the same. But the destination God has for all of us is victory. When you are faithful with what God has placed in your hand, and you don't allow it to become mundane and ordinary, you are living exceptionally. I pray this book is a blessing for you. That it leads you closer to God and nearer to who He made you to be. You are fearfully and wonderfully made.

Live this truth today: You are Exceptional.

Know That You Are Chosen

CHAPTER 1

Put on Your Crown

I have a good friend named Jim, who I've known for many years. Jim told me a story one day that has stayed in my heart ever since. It's the story of when he met his baby sister for the first time. Jim was eight years old. He had been an only child for quite some time, and he was incredibly excited about having a sister. Finally the day came when his father showed up at school and took him out of class to head to the hospital. As his father drove through the streets of the town, parked in the parking lot, and then walked Jim down the long hallways of the hospital, Jim's stomach was rumbling with anticipation. They came to a stop in front of a large nursery window. Jim peered through the glass and saw rows of little babies all bundled up like burritos in their bassinets. A nurse looked up and recognized Jim's father. She smiled and walked out of the nursery, right up to Jim, and bent down to his level. She put her hand on his shoulder and said, "That's your baby sister right there," as she pointed out which baby belonged to his family. As Jim saw her for the first time, his face lit up with joy. There, at last, was his baby sister.

Later that day, recognizing how meeting his sister had made

such a strong impression on his son, Jim's father decided to tell Jim about the day that he was born. He sat down on the sofa right next to his precious boy. He looked into his eyes, making sure he had Jim's full attention, and said, "Jim, when you were born, your mother and I looked through a large nursery window at all the babies, kind of like you and I did today. But something different happened. The nurse told us, 'You can have any baby in this nursery that you want.' We looked at all those babies and we chose you."

You see, Jim is adopted. He didn't know it until that moment. But his father wanted to communicate something very important that day. He wanted him to know this truth: "Jim, you were chosen to be our son. You are so valuable and important to us that we handpicked you to be a part of our family."

Throughout his life, Jim's father always made sure Jim knew how much he was loved and how grateful they were that he was in their family.

That is what your Heavenly Father wants you to know today. You are chosen. Ephesians 1 describes God's great love for you. It says that before the foundation of the world, it pleased God to adopt you as His very own child. He looked through the corridors of time and knew you by name. He handpicked you and brought you into His family through Jesus Christ. He didn't have to adopt you. God chose to adopt you because it pleased Him to call you His own.

> *God chose to adopt you because it pleased Him to call you His own.*

Jim's father would often tell him, "Jim, you were chosen. Don't let anyone tell you any different."

Just like Jim's father reminded him, you need to get up every day and remind yourself that the Creator of the universe chose you and you are valuable to Him.

Don't let your mistakes, failures, or other people talk you out of who you are.

Life has a way of trying to bring us down, discount us, and cause us to forget our true identity. People may judge us, leave us out, and make us feel unqualified. None of that determines who you are—God has already called you and qualified you. You may have made some mistakes. We all have, but that doesn't change your value in the eyes of God. He loves you. Not because of your performance, not because you do everything perfectly, but because you are His child. Take off the negative labels and let go of what people have said to you. Quit beating yourself up for things you can't change. God wants you to move forward in faith, believing that you are chosen, exceptional, and well able to do what He has called you to do.

Know Who You Are

When King David was a young shepherd boy, he was out in the fields tending his father's sheep when the prophet Samuel came to his house to anoint the next king of Israel. Jesse, David's father, brought in all seven of David's older brothers and had them stand in front of Samuel, saying, "Take a look at these fine young men. I believe the king is here." Samuel looked at those tall, strong men and said, "Jesse, the king is not here. Are these all the sons you have?"

I can hear Jesse saying, "Well, there is still the youngest, but he is tending the sheep." Perhaps Jesse didn't think that David was old enough or strong enough to be chosen by God to be king. But when David walked in from the fields, the Lord said to Samuel, "Rise and anoint him. He is the one."

Can you imagine how David felt when he walked in the house and saw all his brothers were first choice and he came in last? David could have been offended, thinking, *Why didn't my dad even consider me?* He could have been upset at the thought of being overlooked or put his head down, thinking, *I guess nobody believes in me. Why should I believe in myself?*

But David didn't have that attitude. He decided, *If I am chosen to be king, I am going to believe that I am a king.* God had already chosen David to be king of Israel long before he was tending his father's sheep out in the fields. Just because David's father didn't recognize the calling on his life didn't change the fact that he was already chosen. His family might have counted him out, but God had already counted him in. They didn't think he looked like the next king. He was too young; he didn't have the training or experience.

But God knew what was on the inside of David. God also knows what's on the inside of you, because He put it there. He knows what you're capable of. If you have ever felt the sting of rejection like David, remember who you are. You are called and chosen by God. Nothing disqualifies you from God's plans, not even a father who doesn't believe in you. Your family may not see your potential, you may not feel appreciated, people at work may not recognize your gifts and talents, friends may leave you out, but don't get discouraged. Like David, God sees you, He knows exactly where you are, and He is calling you in. No one can take your place. Nothing has the power to change God's plan for your life. Don't let other people's actions cause you to question what God has placed on the inside of you. Stand up tall; God's hand is on your life. He has chosen you to do great things. God being for you is more powerful than the world being against you.

> *God being for you is more powerful than the world being against you.*

To be exceptional, you have to know who you are and Whose you are. Now, just because you've been chosen doesn't mean everything happens right away. There is often a period of waiting required. Those times of waiting can be hard. You may feel as though you're out in the shepherd's field today. Don't give up because of challenges or obstacles you may be facing. When David was anointed king, it took him thirteen years before he took his position on the throne. He went back to the shepherd's field. He faced challenges and struggles. He found himself hiding out in caves and running from his predecessor, King Saul, who saw that the "Lord was with David" and was jealous of the favor on David's life and wanted to kill him. There were several times when David could have killed King Saul and vindicated himself for all Saul did to him, but David walked in integrity. He resisted getting even because he knew who he was and he knew he carried an anointing. He was honoring God by protecting what God had placed on his life. David could have given up and wondered why he was facing so many challenges and he could have doubted the call of God on his life. However, he continued to remind himself that he was chosen and did not allow any of the difficulties to change his mind.

Now it's your turn. Do you believe you're chosen, or are you allowing people to talk you out of what God has called you to do? It is so important that you protect what is on your life. You carry a great anointing. Don't try to vindicate yourself and get even. Don't fight battles that aren't yours. Hold your head up high and put your shoulders back. Scripture says you are a "royal priesthood" and "God's special possession." That means you are royalty. Adjust your crown and wear it like you know who you are.

My friend Jim is a successful man today with a beautiful wife and lovely children of his own. He would tell you that one of the greatest things he did for himself was to believe that he was chosen and valuable. He didn't let anyone disqualify him. He remembered his father's words that he was handpicked. In fact, Jim built such a strong foundation of belonging that when his sisters would say to him, "Jim, Mom and Dad love you the most," he would reply, "Of course they do. They had to take you. I was chosen."

Receive this truth in your heart: You are chosen by God. He anointed you and put a calling on your life that is irrevocable. You are exceptional because He made you that way. He declares that His plans for you are for good, to prosper you and not to harm you. He has plans to give you a future and a hope.

God Has Packed Your Bags

I've been blessed to do a lot of traveling in my life. We have participated in over 195 Nights of Hope in arenas all over the country. No matter how many years I've been traveling, I still don't enjoy packing. You'd think I would have grown accustomed to it by now, but I still find myself looking in my bags the night before, thinking, *What have I left out? I don't want to get to where I am going and not have what I need.* Even today, every time I shut my suitcase, I say to myself, "I hope I haven't left anything out."

I think we can all feel that way at times, as if we are missing something or that somehow we are lacking. We wonder if we are talented enough to land that job or receive that promotion. We question if we are smart enough to further our education, pretty enough to marry the man of our dreams, or funny enough for people to like us.

Can I tell you that God has packed your bags and He has left nothing out? You have everything you need to succeed in this life. God does not want us to doubt our worth and abilities. Don't go through life from a position of lack when God has made you more than enough. You have the qualities you need to have successful relationships, a good career, and a strong family. You have the right gifts, the right talents, and the right personality.

In the Bible, there is a man named Jeremiah who God had chosen to be a prophet to the Nations. Jeremiah felt unqualified and didn't know if he had the ability to speak to the people. He questioned God, asking, "How can I speak? I am only a child." Jeremiah didn't think he had what he needed. He felt empty and lacking. God did not leave him in his doubt and disbelief. The Lord told Jeremiah that he was equipped and He would go with him and tell him what to say. God was saying, *Jeremiah, I packed your bags. I chose you and completed you. You are lacking nothing.*

I know it is easy to be like Jeremiah and doubt yourself. When I was a young teenager, my mother wanted me to work with her at my family's jewelry store on the weekends. I didn't feel like I knew enough about fine jewelry and I was sure that I would embarrass myself and my mother if someone asked me a question and I didn't know the answer. But my mother lovingly encouraged me, even as I dragged my feet to the store each weekend. What I didn't realize was that my mother understood my fears and insecurities, but she also knew my gifts and talents. She knew I had everything inside me to succeed, but I had to move forward in faith one step at a time. She trained me through the years, and I began to learn more about the business and feel more confident. I wasn't lacking anything; I had within me the skills to be a good salesperson and spokesperson for the store. It was in that jewelry store that I met the man of my dreams. He came in for a watch battery and I sold him a brand-new watch. Over thirty years later, I am still crazy about him. It looks like Mother knows best after all.

My experience at the jewelry store taught me that God had already packed my bags but it was up to me to unpack what He had put on the inside of me. I had the right gifts and talents for each assignment. It was up to me to push past my fears and insecurities. You too have the right gifts and talents. Your bags have been packed for your special assignments. The problem is too many of us are walking around with our bags packed but unopened. To unpack our bags, we have to push past fears, mistakes, and excuses in order to develop what God has placed in us.

Reaching new levels isn't always easy. Sometimes God will use people, new experiences, and even uncharted territory to nudge us out of our comfort zone. You may feel pressured today. Perhaps you feel some discomfort in your job or with your family. You may be facing a career change or an important decision about your future. Remind yourself that you have everything it takes. Reach deep inside of your bag and unpack what God has placed inside of you. Your faith may feel as if it's being tested and pushed to the extreme. Remember, it's the trial of your faith that brings out the lasting character in your life and builds confidence you cannot attain any other way.

The only difference between a piece of black coal and a precious diamond is the pressure it has endured. It is the pressure that it is under that turns that ordinary piece of coal into a rare and priceless jewel. The truth is the pressure you may be facing isn't going to break you—it's going to make you. It's going to develop you and give you experiences you need

> *Honor God and believe you have what it takes to shine brightly for Him.*

to build your confidence. Honor God and believe you have what it takes to shine brightly for Him.

Some of our talents and gifts are easy to recognize. They're just natural to us. But some things are still on the inside in the form of seeds that need to be developed and nurtured.

I have a huge oak tree in my front yard. It's so beautiful. The branches spread out forty feet, but that tree didn't start out that way. Sixty years ago, it was just a tiny acorn and it didn't look like much. It would have been easy to overlook it, thinking it was insignificant. However, hidden in that tiny acorn was a magnificent tree; it just had to germinate and develop. The gifts and talents God put in you are in seed form, just like that acorn. It's easy to overlook them. They may seem small and ordinary. But when you recognize what God has put in you and see it as significant, you take time to nurture it and develop it. What seems small has incredible potential. Sometimes we pray for an oak tree; we ask for the finished product, but God gives us an acorn.

Are you overlooking gifts and talents, discounting what God has given you? Have a new perspective. Your acorns are full of potential. There's an incredible oak tree in them. It may be small now, but don't discount it. Take time to develop it, nurture it, and watch it grow.

Remember Your True Identity

How you see yourself will determine whether or not you reach your potential. God has created us in His image and crowned us with favor. But too often we allow our limitations and weaknesses, things that have happened to us, how we were treated, and mistakes we've made to distort that image. Rather than seeing ourselves as exceptional, full of potential, chosen by the Most High, we see ourselves as ordinary, thinking we've reached our limits. If my friend Jim would have seen himself as unwanted, if David would have seen himself as not qualified and left out, or if Jeremiah wouldn't have trusted that God would be with him, then we wouldn't be talking about them. So take a moment to really consider: How do you see yourself? Have you taken on an image of yourself that is false, based on something that happened to you rather than the promises of God? We all face disappointments, we all make mistakes, but that's not who we are.

There is a legend about a young queen who was famous throughout the world for her beauty and was loved and admired by her people. One day she was abducted and carried away to another country. With all the confusion and trauma, she was afflicted with amnesia. It was like a switch was flipped and she had no memories of her previous life. She couldn't remember who she was, didn't know her name or where she came from. She ended up living in desperate conditions on the streets. No one who saw her would ever have dreamed that she had royalty in her blood and was a respected and adored queen.

Those who loved her dearly refused to stop looking for her.

Years went by, but her family and friends kept hoping and praying that she was still alive and someone would find her.

One man who loved her deeply and had never lost faith that she was alive finally decided to search for her himself. Traveling far and wide, he eventually found himself searching the streets of a waterfront, where he noticed a woman dressed in dirty rags sitting by the water. Although her face looked beaten up and her hair was tangled and matted, something about her seemed strangely familiar, so before he moved on, he went over and asked her name. She mumbled some incoherent words and looked away. Though he couldn't see her face, there was one thing about her that he had to see. So he asked, "May I see your hands?" He knew the line prints on his beloved queen's hands and would never forget them. As she turned her palms upward, the man stood there, astonished. He whispered, "Helen." She looked at him, bewildered. He said, "You are Helen, queen of our land. You are the queen. Helen, don't you remember?" Suddenly it was as though the switch that had been flipped off had been turned back on again. She remembered who she was. Weeping, she stood up, embraced her friend, and the two of them returned to her homeland, where she once again became the queen she was meant to be.

We are not so different from Helen. We too can develop amnesia through the twists and turns of life. But we cannot forget: We were born into royalty. We were created to reign in life. God crowned us with honor, but we've forgotten who we are. Because of disappointments, unfair situations,

> *We too can develop amnesia through the twists and turns of life. But we cannot forget: We were born into royalty.*

and setbacks, we've taken off our crowns and are living frustrated, stressed out, and far below the privileges that rightfully belong to us, thinking we're average. Like this man did for Helen, I'm here to remind you who you are. You are chosen; you are exceptional; you are handpicked by God. You weren't made to live defeated, depressed, addicted, and unfulfilled. You may have temporarily forgotten what being royalty means, but I believe things are changing, and you are remembering who you really are.

You are exceptional. You have everything you need. Unpack your bags, stir up your faith, and remember that you are royalty. Now, do your part and put your crown back on.

EXCEPTIONAL THOUGHTS

✦ I am a chosen child of God, handpicked by Him and created in His image. He loves me, values me, and has a great purpose for my life. I will not let my mistakes, my failures, or other people talk me out of who I am and Whose I am.

✦ I am loved by God not because of my performance, not because I do everything perfectly, but because I am His child.

✦ I am anointed and have the call of God upon my life to do great things. It doesn't matter whether anyone else recognizes that calling or my gifts and talents. I will stand tall, knowing that God being for me is all I need.

✦ God has packed my bags with everything I need to accomplish the dreams I have for my life. I have the right gifts, the right talents, and the right personality. I am not lacking anything, and I will move forward in faith, knowing that I am fully qualified and well able to do what He has called me to do.

✦ It is up to me to unpack what God has already lovingly placed inside me for my special assignments. I will work with God to develop and bring forth the life He has planned for me.

✦ Because I am God's child, I am royalty, I am His beloved, and I will walk each day knowing my true identity. I will not allow things that have happened to me, how I was treated, or mistakes I've made to distort that image.

CHAPTER 2

Speak the Amen

I didn't know I married a pastor. When Joel and I were first married, he worked behind the scenes in his father's ministry, and we never imagined that we would take over the church when his father passed away. Joel and I have always loved Lakewood Church and his family, and we knew that we would always be part of the ministry in some capacity, but we never envisioned leading the church.

Of course God had different plans.

I never thought I could stand up in front of the congregation and give a message every week. I remember the first time Joel's father, John, asked me to speak. He wanted me to encourage the congregation before prayer in a Sunday morning service. During worship, I had my eyes closed, singing and praising, when I opened my eyes and saw John had turned around in his seat and was looking at me intently. He asked quietly, "Victoria, do you want to do the prayer time segment?"

I know I must have looked at him in shock. He was not talking about next week or next month, but at the end of the song that was just about to finish. I stood there, stunned. I had never given him any impression that I wanted to do the prayer time, so I didn't understand why he was asking me. Laughing nervously, I said, "Daddy O, I don't think so." He smiled gently, as only he could do, turned around, and didn't say another word about it.

When I returned home that afternoon, I couldn't shake this feeling of unease. I struggled with the fact that I had said no. I kept thinking about what might have caused Daddy O to ask me in the first place. He obviously believed in me, but I didn't even have the courage to believe in myself. The more I thought about it, the more I realized that I was mad at myself. I felt frustrated and disappointed because of my lack of courage. Now, I felt nervous any time I had to pray in front of people, even a small group, but somehow that no just didn't sit right with me. I knew there was a yes in my heart. I wanted to rise to the occasion; the problem was the yes was buried beneath the fear and insecurity. My yes had been drowned out because I was uncertain and I didn't know if I could do it.

Have you ever said no to an opportunity because you didn't feel prepared or you thought someone else was more qualified? You really wanted to say yes, but maybe you were just fearful because you didn't know how it would turn out. Maybe you said no to an opportunity because you didn't know if you had the time or the talent. Maybe you said no to a promotion because you were unsure of your skills. We have all said no to things in our lives, but we can't let fear of failure or lack of experience talk us out of our yes. Making excuses will keep us from growing and experiencing

> *We have all said no to things in our lives, but we can't let fear of failure or lack of experience talk us out of our yes.*

new opportunities. If we are going to accomplish our dreams and reach the fullness of our destiny, we must press past our excuses and put aside the no, grab hold of our yes, and take bold steps of faith.

When God told Moses that he was being sent to deliver Israel from the captivity of the pharaoh, the first thing he said was, "I can't do it." He began to tell God all the reasons why he couldn't do it; he was slow with his speech, stuttered his words, and wanted someone else to speak for him. Finally, God asked Moses, "Who made your mouth?" God was reminding Moses who packed his bags. God wanted him to get his thinking straight, to know he had everything he needed to get the job done. Then God said to him, "Now go. I will help you speak and teach you what to say."

Like Moses, sometimes opportunities come our way and the first thing that comes to mind is *I can't*. It's not that we don't want to; it's just that we can become overwhelmed with feelings of fear and insecurity. We begin to think we don't have the resources or the ability. God is saying the same thing to us today that He said to Moses. "Go, and I will help you. Go, and I will teach you." Our God is an "I can" God, and He wants us to be "I can" people. The apostle Paul says, "I can do all things through Christ who strengthens me." Just as God taught Moses, He wants to teach us to think "I can" thoughts.

I can break bad habits. I can have good relationships. I can forgive. I can be successful. I can overcome. I can do all things through Christ.

After that Sunday, I wrestled with my no for several days before I finally came to the conclusion "If Daddy O ever asks me again, I'm going to say yes." I committed in my heart to saying yes the next time he asked. I even started thinking of what I could say during that prayer time, because I was determined to stick to my yes. I wanted to feel comfortable knowing I had something prepared in advance. So when I went to church that next Sunday, and the worship song began, I put my hands up, shut my eyes, and said, "God, not today, please. Don't let it be this Sunday he asks me." While it wasn't that day, eventually the day did come when Daddy O finally asked me again. I mustered up the courage and I stuck to my yes, and I believe that because I did, God gave me the grace to get up and do it.

Taking that one step of faith broke the limitation in my mind. Every time after that I gained a little more experience, had a little more confidence, and my yes became stronger. When I began stirring up my gifts and pushing past fear, pushing past the doubt, believing that God put everything I needed on the inside of me, it led me to eventually stand up on the platform and give my first sermon. If I hadn't been determined to uncover the yes that was hiding within me, I would have missed so many opportunities down the road.

You see, God was up to something. I didn't know at the time what was in my future, but God did. He knew that many years later I would be up on the platform in front of people every Sunday. He was preparing me. He had already called me and chosen me for the task; I just needed to take that first step of faith toward my destiny.

Jesus said, "I am the vine; you are the branches" (John 15:5). When you stay connected to Christ, you are connected to the power source. But you have to let go of "I can't" before you can to take hold of the "I can." With God, you can move past those limited mind-sets that are trying to hold you back and walk through those doors of opportunity that God has opened for you.

God is up to something in your life. He knows what is in your future. He is preparing you and getting you ready. If there is a yes in your heart, it is because God placed it there. It's time to act on your yes. It's not in you by accident. Let the yes drown out the no that is trying to talk you out of what God has put in your heart. He wants to do something in your

> *God has an assignment with your name on it. It is an assignment He wants you to accomplish for Him.*

life that seems impossible. He wants to take you to new levels in your faith so you can rise higher and go beyond where you are right now. Let go of the insecurities that try to hold you back. God has an assignment with your name on it. It is an assignment He wants you to accomplish for Him.

God Will Use You

You may know the story of Abraham and Sarah and how God promised them that they were going to have a child. When He made this promise, they were well past the age of bearing children. It seemed impossible. Sarah didn't see how she could ever have a baby, so she began to assume that God's promise would come to them through someone else. In fact, she went so far as to take matters into her own hands and told her husband to sleep with her handmaiden, Hagar. Her handmaiden gave birth to a son, but as we find out later, that child wasn't the promised child. God spoke the promise to Sarah, not to Hagar, her handmaiden.

That was Sarah's assignment. God was saying, *Sarah, I didn't put the promise in someone else. I put the promise in you.*

God continued to tell Abraham and Sarah that they would have a child, and Sarah continued to doubt that it would come to pass. Sarah even laughed at the idea. She didn't believe that she had the ability to bring forth the child that God said they would have. She considered her age and the fact that it hadn't happened yet; she was looking at all the wrong things. However, the fact remained: God had chosen her. Twenty years later, at the age of ninety, against all odds, she gave birth to the son God had promised and they named him Isaac. God is the God of all possibilities. Even when you can't see how it can happen, God has a way.

Are you telling yourself you can't accomplish your dreams, you don't have the connections, you're too old, it's too late, you've made too many mistakes? You may feel like the odds are against you, but what God has promised will come to pass. It's not going to come through other people; it's going to come through you. You may not see how it could happen, but God always has a way. God has already packed your bags for every assignment that He will ever give you. You don't need anyone else to give birth to the promise that God put in your heart.

> *You don't need anyone else to give birth to the promise that God put in your heart.*

Don't allow your no to cause you to look to other people to do the things God wants you to do. Like Sarah, it may take time or like Moses, you may feel unqualified. Like me, you may not feel ready. You may not see how God could use you or how it could happen, but God wants to work in you and through you. You need to get into agreement with God. Say what God says about you. You can do all things through Christ. You are well able to accomplish your dreams. You can have a strong family. You can have a successful career. You can walk in the blessings of God. He is waiting on your yes. Scripture says, "For no matter how many promises God has made, they are 'Yes' in Christ. And so through him the 'Amen' is spoken by us to the glory of God" (2 Cor. 1:20). We speak the amen. *Amen* means "so be it." Get into agreement with God and be willing to take a risk and step out in faith. God has chosen you and you are exceptional.

A man in the Bible named Gideon had great potential, but he couldn't see it in himself. One day he was threshing wheat in a wine press to hide it from the Midianites who were taking over the land and stealing everything that the Israelites possessed. An angel of the Lord appeared to him and said, "Gideon, the Lord is with you, you mighty man of fearless courage."

Gideon stopped what he was doing and questioned the angel. "Sir," he said, "if the Lord is with us, why has all this happened to us?" The angel ignored his lack of faith and responded, "Go in the strength you have and save Israel out of Midian's hand. Am I not sending you?" Gideon replied, "Wait a minute, how can I do that? My family is the poorest in Manasseh, we don't amount to anything, and I am the least in my father's house."

God is telling Gideon that he has been chosen to save his people, and all Gideon can do is find excuses for why it should be somebody else. There's such a contrast between how Gideon saw himself and how God saw him. Gideon thought he was weak, incapable, unqualified, and from the wrong family. He was full of fear. But God saw him as a fearless, courageous champion. He knew Gideon had the strength and ability and was up to the task.

Gideon, like many of us, needed some convincing before he was willing to say yes. He asked the angel to provide a sign that he was in fact a messenger of God. When he saw the "proof" that God sent him, he finally got in agreement with God. He took hold of God's strength, went out, and won the victory.

God is saying to us what He said to Gideon: You're a person of fearless courage. He's calling out the great things on the inside of you. Don't let your own voice of doubt drown out the voice of God. Shake off whatever's trying to hold you back and let the voice of God come booming through loud and clear. You may feel weak, but your weakness can be turned into strength when you get in agreement with God. Believe that you have what it takes and give God your yes.

> *Don't let your own voice of doubt drown out the voice of God.*

Stir Up Your Faith

The other day I had such a craving for a glass of cold chocolate milk. I used to drink it all the time when I was a kid. So I went into the kitchen, poured a cold glass of milk, added two scoops of chocolate, and stirred it up. It was so delicious—as good as I remembered. But then I heard my phone ringing in the other room. I put down my glass and went to answer the phone.

After I finished my phone call, I went back into the kitchen to finish drinking the chocolate milk when I noticed that the milk and the chocolate had separated. All the chocolate had settled to the bottom of the glass.

Though we don't always realize it, sometimes that is what can happen in our lives. Our dreams and desires can sink to the bottom of our glass. Because of disappointments and challenges, or things taking longer than we expected, we can become separated from the joy and passion we once had. The goals we were so excited about at one time—to start our business, to get out of debt, to be healthy again—can be pushed down because of the pressures of life. If you have ever felt that way, separated from your goals or your dreams, the good news is you are still full of gifts and talents and you have the ability to fulfill those dreams and accomplish what God placed in your heart. That day in the kitchen, I took my spoon and stirred up my chocolate milk again and it tasted as good as ever. I want to encourage you to take out your God spoon and begin to stir up what's inside of you. Stir up your potential, stir up your dreams, and stir up your passion. It can be as good as ever. God didn't create you to just endure life, but to enjoy life; not to be average but to be exceptional.

The apostle Paul had a young protégé named Timothy. He noticed Timothy was struggling and going through challenges much like those we all face; he was feeling discouraged and inferior, thinking he wasn't up for the task. Maybe he was comparing himself to Paul. When he looked at Paul's life, his talent, his leadership skills, his ability to speak and write so effectively, Timothy felt like he would never measure up. He was looking outward instead of inward. That's why Paul said, "Timothy, stir up the gift of God within you" (see 2 Tim. 1:6). Notice Paul's words: *within you*. He knew what God had placed inside Timothy. He knew he had the gifts, the talents, the determination, the favor, and the wisdom. He just needed to believe they were in him and stir them up.

Don't let your dreams, desires, or your goals fall to the bottom of the glass. You are full of potential. God has put amazing things in you. You are full of ideas, creativity, and ability. God is

saying to you, *Stir up what's in you. Let that yes rise to the surface.*
Start believing you can accomplish what's in your heart. You're not lacking. You didn't get shortchanged. God wouldn't be asking you to do something if you didn't already have the ability to succeed.

> God wouldn't be asking you to do something if you didn't already have the ability to succeed.

Like Gideon, you will see God's hand of favor and blessing, and go farther than you ever imagined.

Destiny Moments Are in Your Future

There are times in our lives when we feel like we're not enough, when we are at a disadvantage, when we don't know the right people, or we can't seem to get the right breaks. When we get anxious, we need to be on the lookout for ways that God is helping us. Don't live frustrated. Trust that God is in control, that He's not only directing your steps, but also directing the steps of the people you need. He's putting you in the right place at the right time. Live in peace, knowing that the Creator of the universe has ordained your future.

> Live in peace, knowing that the Creator of the universe has ordained your future.

At the appointed time, you'll come into destiny moments, where God thrusts you to new levels.

I have a good friend who was a TV news reporter when she was in her early twenties. And because she struggled with really bad rosacea, she always had to put on a lot of makeup to feel presentable in front of the camera. One day while she was anchoring the news, the heat from the hot lights on the set caused her to perspire. When she wiped the sweat off her face, her makeup came off as well, leaving an embarrassing patch of red skin for everyone to see. My friend tried many different kinds of makeup to see if she could find some that would truly last all day, but she was always disappointed.

She was so frustrated that she decided to try and create the makeup herself. She quit her job as a reporter and threw herself into research. Eventually, she developed a product that she really liked and believed would be successful. To produce this makeup, she needed financial backing. She and her husband went to bank after bank, but they were turned down again and again. Eventually, they received a small amount of money from a few friends and family members, but ultimately they realized that to launch the company they would have to do it primarily on their own. They created a website so they could get their product out to the public. It was up for weeks and weeks with no activity, no orders. Finally, an order came through. She went running to her husband and said, "Look, we got our first order." He said, "No, that was me. I was just testing the website."

My friend knew that to launch successfully, she needed to get on a network like QVC or into beauty stores like Ulta or Sephora. For years, she sent them all product and tried to meet with representatives, but no one ever reached out after those meetings. Finally, she and her husband were down to their last thousand dollars in the bank, and they had one last cosmetics convention that they planned to attend. All of the major companies were there. All my friend could afford was a tiny three-foot booth. Right across the aisle stood the enormous booth of QVC. After a couple of hours and after hundreds of people had passed by her booth, one woman stopped and seemed to really want to understand the product and my friend's story. It happened to be one of the on-air personalities from QVC who had been on the network for over seventeen years. My friend introduced herself and starting talking about her makeup. She even went so far as to show the woman the concealer and put it on right there. The woman left with her product, and my friend prayed that this was the open door that she needed so desperately.

A few weeks later she received a call from QVC. This woman had told the network executives about this young lady she met and her cosmetics company, and to give her a chance. They offered her one ten-minute slot. If she sold out her product, they would invite her back. If she didn't, that was it.

My friend couldn't believe it. She knew this was the moment she had been praying for. The even more trying part was my friend had to bring in over six thousand units of her concealer to sell in just ten minutes. And if it didn't sell, she would have to take it all back. Everything was on the line.

Finally the day arrived. When she got to QVC, she practiced her lines and went out onstage. As the lights glared in her eyes, she talked enthusiastically about this makeup line and why she had created it. It felt like ten seconds instead of ten minutes, but all of a sudden her time was up, and at the very same moment that the clock ran out, a SOLD OUT sign flashed across the screen. She looked at the host, and tears began to stream down her face. She had done it.

After that day, they gave her another ten-minute slot, and then another. Today, my friend, Jamie Kern, the founder of IT Cosmetics, goes on QVC two hundred times a year. Her company has become one of the largest cosmetic companies in the world and is now also sold in Sephora and Ulta Beauty. Eight years after she founded her company, L'Oréal acquired IT Cosmetics for a huge sum of money, making Jamie the first female CEO in L'Oréal's hundred-plus-year history.

Years later, when Jamie was thanking the woman who truly launched her career, she asked her why she did it. What was it about the concealer that convinced her that Jamie's line would be a success? This woman said, "Well, I liked your product but it wasn't about the makeup. When I saw you that day, I felt like God said to me, 'Go help that young lady.' Once I met you, I knew you'd be good on the air. And so I told the executives about you. But you know what, Jamie? You did all the rest."

Even when you feel like nothing is working out, and things are taking so much longer than you expected, God has the right people lined up for you. He's reaching out to people who you don't know anything about. Doors are going to open that you couldn't open. You don't have to worry, trying to constantly make things happen. It's already lined up. What you need is en route. A destiny moment is right around the corner. At the right time you're going to see divine connections. Like Jamie, people will want to be good to you. You may not know the right people but God does. He's directing your steps and the people you need.

> *You may not know the right people but God does. He's directing your steps and the people you need.*

Stay in faith; believe that He is working behind the scenes and He will open the right doors at the right time and get you to where you need to be. When you speak the "amen," you stay in agreement with God and keep your faith alive. Because your trust is in God, you partner with Him, and together you'll do amazing things.

Shake the Bridge

What buried yes is seeking to rise to the surface? Many of the saints initially said no. Sarah turned to her handmaiden. Gideon thought God should choose someone else. Moses said, "I can't." Just like my father-in-law asked me a second time, God's going to ask you again. He's not going to hold your no against you. He's going to ask you again. Why don't you quit wrestling with that no and just say yes to God? God has given you some assignments that only you can do, and He wants you to bring them to pass on this earth.

To speak the amen means that we say yes to God even when things take a long time and when others don't understand what we are doing. We still say yes to God. Noah is a great example of this. When God asked him to build a huge ark, people thought Noah was crazy. Every step of the way, people discounted him and said, "Noah has lost his mind. What is he doing?" But Noah kept working at what God had instructed him to do. He didn't let people's ridicule and unbelief change his yes. He stirred up his faith. He stayed in agreement with God.

There are always going to be opportunities and reasons to give up. Time passes, and we wonder, *Is it really you, God? Is this delay your denial? Should I let it go and give up?* People may criticize you. They don't understand what God has spoken to you. The Bible says to hold fast to your profession of faith. That means hold tight to your yes and stay in agreement with God. You need to hold fast to His promises and keep marching on with God, because He will give you the ability to fullfill the plans He has for your life.

When my kids were younger, they used to watch this cartoon about a mouse and an elephant. In one of the episodes, this tiny little mouse and his friend, a huge elephant, went for a walk. They admired the flowers and birds along the way. Soon they came to a rickety old bridge that crossed a rapidly flowing river. As they crossed the bridge, it trembled and shook and swayed under the weight of the elephant. When they were safely on the other side, the mouse was so excited. He looked up at his elephant friend and said ever so proudly, "Wow, we really shook that bridge, didn't we?"

When you take hold of God's strength, you're like that little mouse. You may feel small in comparison to what you are facing, but you have to remember that with Almighty God, you have the strength of an elephant. Hold fast to His promises and you will look up and say, "Wow, God, we really shook some bridges, didn't we?"

EXCEPTIONAL THOUGHTS

✦ When opportunities come my way, I won't let my fear of failure or my insecurities or my lack of experience drown out the yes God put in my heart. I will stay connected to Christ, my power source, and walk through the doors of opportunity He opens for me.

✦ I am full of ideas, creativity, and ability. I will stir up my faith and let my dreams and my passion rise to the surface again, believing that God put them there for a reason and He will bring them to pass.

✦ I will take hold of the phrase "I can" even when I can't see how it can happen. God will find a way and is preparing a destiny moment for me right now.

✦ I will not look to other people to do the things God wants me to do. I don't need anyone else to give birth to the promise that God put in my heart.

✦ God says I am a person of fearless courage. I will not let my own voice of doubt drown out the voice of God. I will hold fast to God's promises and keep marching on with Him. I can do all things through Christ.

✦ I will be on the lookout for ways that God is helping me. I believe He is directing not only my steps but also the steps of the people I need. At the appointed time, I will come into destiny moments where God thrusts me to new levels.

Lift Up Your Eyes

CHAPTER 3

Set Your Eyes on the Promises

The other day, I heard a story about a man who was feeling down and discouraged. After several weeks of being in a state of despair, he went to one of his pastors at the church and said, "Pastor, I hate to bother you, but you know, right now, I feel like my life is a wreck. There are disappointments all around, and I don't understand why this is happening to me. I don't have anything good going on in my life."

The pastor invited the man into his office, pulled out a legal pad of paper, drew a line down the center of it, and said, "Okay, I hear how frustrated you are and that things are not going your way right now. Let's take a moment to inventory your life, as it stands. On the right side, I'm going to write down all your assets—all the things that are good in your life. On the left side, I'm going to list all your challenges, your problems, and your disappointments. Sound good?"

The man dropped his head and said, "I'm not going to have anything to even list on the right side. There is nothing right in my life."

The pastor nodded his head with understanding. "I get it.

Listen, let's just go ahead and make our lists. By the way, I've been wanting to say that I am so sorry to hear that your wife passed away."

The man looked up in surprise and protested, "My wife didn't pass away. She's alive and healthy." The pastor smiled and said, "Oh, really?" He wrote on the right side of the page, *Wife, alive and healthy*. Then he said, "But it is a shame that your house burned down." The man shook his head and blurted out, "What are you talking about? My house didn't burn down." The pastor smiled again and said, "Oh, my mistake." Then he wrote on the right side of the page, *Living in a house*.

The man looked at his pastor in confusion. "Where are you getting all this ridiculous information?"

The pastor smiled at him and didn't say anything. After a few seconds, the man recognized what was going on. By the time they finished their session, the man had a long list of blessings on the right side of his page. He soon realized that he was looking at the wrong things and gained a new perspective. He walked out of the church with a different attitude and a spring in his step.

What we choose to focus on can make all the difference in our lives. Through that simple activity, that man realized he could change his perspective by changing his focus. It's like the classic question: *Is the glass half full or half empty?* The amount of water in the glass is the same, no matter how you answer. It's just how one chooses to see the amount of water in the glass that changes the perspective.

How are you viewing your life today? Does it feel half empty or half full? Did you get up this morning ready to embrace the day? Or did you wake up weary, focused on the trials that you may be facing and the frustrations that lie in your path?

To be exceptional means you are intentional with your attitude. Looking for what's right in your life and being grateful for what you have. When we look for God's goodness and set our eyes on His promises, our thoughts will shift from defeat to victory.

Rearrange Your Thoughts

A few years ago, every time I walked into my living room, I'd think, *I don't like the way this room looks. I wish I could just get rid of all this furniture and start over. That would be so amazing.* As the days went by, any time I walked past that room, my attitude was sour. I would feel frustrated and I could hear myself complaining about it on the inside. Now, this was my living room. It was in the center of my house. I couldn't move that room. I couldn't avoid seeing it several times a day.

One day, when I realized that I probably wouldn't be getting new furniture anytime soon, I decided it was time to rearrange the furniture I did have. There was no one around to help me, so I put towels under the legs of the couch and began pulling the couch around, trying it in different locations. Then I moved a chair and a side table, and I even rearranged the lamps. When I finally finished, I stepped back, and to my delight, my perception of the room had changed completely. I stood there thinking: *I like this room. It looks really good.* I had a whole new attitude toward my furniture. I went and made myself a big glass of iced tea and sat on the couch to enjoy the view. I realized I had never seen that piece of furniture from that perspective. I thought, *It is so pretty. And look how the colors in that picture really pop next to those chairs.*

I was able to have a fresh attitude toward my living room and see it differently because I rearranged it. Now when I walk past that room, I feel gratitude instead of frustration.

Sometimes we need to do the same thing to our thoughts. When you feel down and discouraged, you need to pay attention to what you are thinking. Just as I rearranged my furniture, we need to rearrange our thinking so that we can see things from a new perspective. So often we don't pay attention to the way our thoughts affect our attitudes. Don't let your thoughts push you around; push your thoughts around and be made new in the attitude of your mind. Scripture says put on a fresh new attitude everyday.

> *We need to rearrange our thinking so that we can see things from a new perspective.*

Have a Winning Attitude

You have heard the saying "Your attitude determines your altitude." It means that our attitudes have a direct correlation with the level of success in our lives. In fact, a study came out from Stanford University about how powerful a positive attitude can be. They found that a positive attitude can be just as important a predictor of success as your IQ.[1] So while you may not be able to control your IQ, you do have the ability to impact your attitude. In the same way, we can't always control our circumstances, but we can control our attitude about our circumstances. When you take charge of your thoughts and attitudes, your life will go to new levels. Empower your life with positive thoughts of faith.

Joshua and Caleb provide a powerful example of how to ignite your faith with the right thoughts and attitudes. The Israelites had recently left Egypt under the leadership of Moses, where they had been living in bondage under Pharaoh. God delivered them with the promise of restoring Israel to the Land of Canaan, the Promised Land, which flowed with the abundance of provision. As they traveled to this new land, Moses sent twelve spies ahead of the tribe, including Joshua and Caleb, on an exploratory mission to scout out the Land of Canaan and find out as much as they could before the Israelites entered the land to take it as their own. He instructed them to bring back some of the fruit of the land for everyone to see.

The twelve spies were in Canaan for forty days and then returned to the Israelites with a huge cluster of grapes and amazing pomegranates and figs. Everyone marveled over the bounty, realizing the land was rich in produce and indeed flowing with abundance as they had heard. However, the rejoicing didn't last long, because ten of the spies began to talk about the problems they saw, spreading a bad report throughout the whole camp: "There are giants in the land. The cities have huge walls around them. We'll never be able to conquer those people. They are bigger than we are. In fact, we look like grasshoppers in our own sights, and so we are in their sight."

Joshua and Caleb, hearing the negative report, spoke up, saying, "If the Lord delights in us then He will bring us into the land and give it to us." They saw that the land was good. They also saw the fortified cities and how big the men were. However, they chose not to focus on the stature of the people; they chose to focus on the size of their God. They saw how the Lord was with them, protecting and enabling them to go through the land for forty days unharmed. They remembered how God had parted the sea as they were leaving Egypt and drowned their enemies. They believed that if God had promised them this land, He would bring them into the land and give them the victory.

Ten spies chose to see the glass half empty whereas two spies saw the glass half full.

A negative attitude can have devastating consequences. The report of the ten spies spread throughout the tribe. The Bible says the Israelites wept the whole night through. You would think they would remember the many miracles they had seen God perform, but they didn't. They took on the attitude of the negative report, thinking God had left them at the threshold of the Promised Land. They began to constantly grumble and complain, denying God's power in their lives. And because of their attitudes, they wandered in the wilderness for forty years, and no one over the age of twenty entered the Promised Land—with two exceptions.

Joshua and Caleb, whose faith never wavered, made it to the Promised Land. They had what the Bible referred to as "a different spirit." They chose to believe and obey, not according to what they saw, but according to what God said. While the rest of the adults died in the wilderness, Joshua and Caleb thrived because of their spirit of faith. After forty years, they were strong enough to lead the next generation into the land God had promised.

> *When you have the right attitude, you can look at your situation, no matter how challenging it may seem, and make it through by choosing to set your eyes on the promises of God.*

When you have the right attitude, you can look at your situation, no matter how challenging it may seem, and make it through by choosing to set your eyes on the promises of God. When you choose to see through your eyes of faith, not fear, you will come out of the wilderness moments stronger and more determined than you were before.

At eighty-five years old, Caleb declared, "I feel better than I ever have. I am as strong today as I was forty-five years ago, and I'm ready to take this land and destroy the giants" (see Josh. 14:10–12).

As they led the next generation into the Promised Land, Joshua's motto empowered them to understand the importance of a good attitude: "Choose you this day whom you will serve." He wanted them to know the choice was theirs. They didn't have to follow the crowd or the latest trends. They could choose what they wanted to focus on in life. As he encouraged them with his wisdom, he added: "As for me and my house, we're going to serve the Lord."

When you choose to serve the Lord, you quiet the discouraging voices that try to come against you by looking through your eyes of faith, not fear. You choose to believe that God is a Mighty God and He will do what He promised. He has already disarmed the power of the enemy. Don't focus on the giants, feeling overwhelmed by your circumstances, but rather focus on the promises of God that guarantee the victory.

We can't always control our environment, but we can control our thoughts and attitudes. When we put on that winning attitude, it will shift the way we approach even the most challenging situations.

> *When we put on that winning attitude, it will shift the way we approach even the most challenging situations.*

I have a friend who says she has a "lucky" shirt. And for every important business meeting, every presentation, every situation where she wants to feel confident that everything is going to go her way, she wears this shirt. Now, there is nothing special about that shirt. It isn't about the shirt, it is about the thoughts and attitude she has when she wears that shirt. She thinks, *Everything is going to go my way today. I'm going to succeed because I have my lucky shirt on.* But it's not the shirt that creates success. Her thoughts create a winning attitude. Her thoughts give her confidence that she has what it takes to succeed.

Every day you need to wake up believing that God has clothed you with His power. And that His goodness and mercy follow you all the days of your life. Then you will have the courage and boldness to move forward in faith as a victor and not a victim.

Lifting the Veil

In the book of Genesis, Abraham was called by God to go on a journey of faith. What God promised Abraham looked impossible. Abraham moved forward in faith with his eyes on God. When God said, "Leave your father's house," Abraham did as God instructed. He left the only home he knew with his family and his nephew Lot.

At the next stage of the journey, Lot and Abraham had to separate, because their possessions became so great that the land couldn't sustain both of them. Abraham was disappointed, but he trusted God. He told Lot to choose which direction he wanted to go. Lot looked at all the land and chose for himself a land that was flourishing with beauty and opportunity. When Abraham looked west, to where he was set to go, it didn't look like the lush land that Lot had chosen, it was much less desirable. It was at this point God spoke to Abraham and said, "Lift up your eyes and look from the place where you are. All the land that you can see, I will give it to you and your offspring forever" (see Gen. 13:14–15). Abraham had to lift his eyes from the disappointment and challenges of where he was and begin to look to the new things God wanted to show him.

It's interesting that the name *Lot* means "veil." When the two men parted ways, God lifted the veil from Abraham's eyes and he was able to see God in new ways. God wanted to reveal Himself to Abraham. As Abraham lifted his eyes, and as he looked beyond where he was, he began to see his destiny unfold. With lifted eyes he could look beyond where he was to the new places God was taking him.

In the same way, Scripture talks about how the veil has been lifted from our eyes. It has been torn in two by the power of Christ. Along your journey, God wants to show you things you haven't seen before. He wants to reveal Himself in powerful ways. He is saying the same thing to you that He said to Abraham, "Lift your eyes to Me, and I will show you the great things I am doing in your life."

It's easy to focus on what didn't work out, what didn't happen, the mistakes we've made, or what someone else did to us. Take your eyes off the problems that are trying to weigh you down and hold you back, and instead lift up your eyes and look at the promises of God. We can't set our eyes on the problems; we have to set our eyes on the promises. That's how we're going to rise above where we are right now. When we look for God, He always shows up.

> *We can't set our eyes on the problems; we have to set our eyes on the promises.*

A friend of mine was sitting in the waiting room at a lawyer's office. She was feeling insecure and stressed out, trying to remember all the questions she had for the

> *When we look for God, He always shows up.*

lawyer and praying that she would have the wisdom to remember and understand his answers. She felt overwhelmed and unsure in her abilities. She prayed, "God, how am I going to do this?" Reflecting back on a conversation we had, she remembered that when we feel overcome by a situation, we need to shift our eyes off the problem and look up to God. And so she did just that. She opened her eyes and looked up, and right above the door to her lawyer's office was a sign that said: PRAYER CHANGES EVERYTHING.

My friend had been to this office many times before and had never seen that sign. She knew it was a message from God, that He was by her side and she was not alone. With her head held high, she walked into that meeting with confidence and the assurance that God was with her. She asked all the questions she needed and understood the answers with total clarity.

God knows that there are times when we feel unsure or insecure, and overwhelmed by our circumstances. When we look to God in every situation, we must trust that He will show up and make a way for us to overcome our difficulties. God wants to build confidence in us so we can have faith that He will always be there for us.

Trust the Journey

When God called Abraham to leave his country, He said, "I will make you into a great nation, and I will bless you...all peoples on earth will be blessed through you" (Gen. 12:2–3). At that time his name was still Abram and he was childless. Many years later, God changed his name to Abraham, meaning "the father of many nations," but he still didn't have any children. He didn't look anything like the man God promised he would be, but God's promises are spoken in the unseen realm. That's why God lifts the veil so that we can get a glimpse of what He's doing. We won't always see every step of the way, but He shows us enough to comfort, encourage, and empower us to move forward.

> *We won't always see every step of the way, but He shows us enough to comfort, encourage, and empower.*

God's promises are progressive, meaning they unfold in His timing. They may not be seen yet, but trust God's timing and you will become everything you were meant to be.

I have two beautiful lemon trees in my backyard, and they're full of fruit right now. I was in the backyard with a friend the other day and when we were walking by the lemon trees, she stopped and paused for a minute and then said, "Those are the most amazing lime trees I have ever seen."

I started to laugh. "Those aren't lime trees. They're lemon trees."

She said, "Those are lime trees . . . They look like limes to me."

I nodded and said, "They look like limes, but the fruit on those trees is still in process. They're not finished yet. They're green now and look like limes, but they're going to turn yellow in just a matter of time."

Hebrews 6 says that we inherit the promises of God through faith and patience (see v. 12). Just like those lemons are in process, you are becoming everything God wants you to be. You may not be where you want to be; your seeds of greatness are still developing. Don't devalue your journey or forget the purpose of the process. The process is what builds your strength. The process is what develops you. The process is what makes you become all God's called you to be.

46   Lift Up Your Eyes

All along Abraham's journey, he walked through the process, trusting God, overcoming challenges, and growing strong in his faith. If you go through the process correctly, you too will become strong in your faith, living with purpose and fulfilling your destiny. Abraham was one hundred years old before he received his promised child, Isaac. Through the process, he discovered the character of God. He saw God's faithfulness and God's provision. He came to know God in a way he had never known before.

You're in the process, and you are becoming everything God created you to be. If you find yourself consumed with a problem today, or going through a transition in your life, wondering how something is going to work out, it's time to lift your eyes from the problem and set your eyes on the promises. Don't let negative attitudes fill your heart and convince you that everything is going wrong in your life. Where you are right now is not your final destination. Beyond this place are greater heights, greater victories, greater strength, and a greater anointing. If you won't settle where you are, if you'll continue the process, you will become like Abraham and you will see God's faithfulness in your life.

> *Where you are right now is not your final destination.*

Are you living with lifted eyes? Are you focused on how big the problem is or on how big our God is? Are you trusting God even when it doesn't make sense? He's directing your steps. He knows what you need. Keep walking in obedience and keep looking up. Every time Abraham needed something, he looked up and found God. He saw God's promise in the multitude of stars in the sky, and God's provision through a ram in the bush. If you keep your eyes lifted, God will show up in your life.

This is what David did. He says, "I lift up my eyes to the mountains—where does my help come from? My help comes from the LORD, the Maker of heaven and earth" (Ps. 121:1–2). David knew that when he looked up at those mountains around Jerusalem, the blessings of God were there. That he had everything he needed—the provisions of God, the healing of God, the protection of God—because God had promised it.

God has amazing things in store for you, but you have to make a choice: "Am I going to look at my circumstances and get stuck, or am I going to believe that on the other side of my circumstances, God has greater things?" God is saying to you today, "Look up. I made you for more." Don't feel discouraged with where you are. This is not your final destination. You may be green, but you will turn yellow. You may be Abram but you're becoming Abraham. You can't rush the process. Lift up your eyes and you'll see the greatness of our God. He always leads us to the Promised Land.

EXCEPTIONAL THOUGHTS

+ My thoughts have incredible power. I will not allow myself to be at the mercy of negative thoughts, letting them dictate my attitude and my day. I choose to push my thoughts around so I can see all the good that God has placed in my life.

+ I can't control my environment, but I can control my thoughts. I will not be a victim of my circumstances. I choose to serve the Lord and put on a winning attitude that shifts the way I approach even the most challenging situations.

+ I will not set my eyes on problems, on my circumstances, or whatever is trying to weigh me down and hold me back. I will lift up my eyes and see the greatness of my God.

+ I will set my focus on the promises of God and give them my attention today. No matter what giants I face, His promises are greater. I choose to believe that He will do what He's promised and that His promises guarantee my victory.

+ I will have a different spirit, an excellent spirit, and I believe that God is a big God.

+ God is not finished with me. I'm in the process of becoming all He made me to be. I will look up toward the future He has promised me and stop seeking to rush the process. God's timing is perfect and He knows what He's doing.

CHAPTER 4

Align Yourself with God

When I was a little girl, I loved to go to Galveston Beach with my family. We would pack up the car and drive to the coast. We'd find a good spot, set up our blanket, and raise a red umbrella to shade us from the sun. As my parents sat down under the umbrella and grabbed cold drinks from the ice chest, I would run off to the water, where I would play for hours, getting lost in my thoughts and dancing in the waves.

Out from the shore, there are a series of sandbars that run parallel to the beach. One afternoon, I was feeling bold and decided to swim out to the second sandbar. I left the first sandbar near the beach and swam through the deep part of the water until I reached the second sandbar. Even though I was pretty far from the shore, I was now standing in knee-deep water. I was quite proud of myself, having braved the deep water to get there and I wanted my family to see me. I turned around, expecting to see my family under the familiar red umbrella, and while I could see lots of families, I couldn't find mine. I couldn't see that red umbrella.

I tried not to panic, but as a little girl, I knew I needed to find my family. I swam as quickly as I could back to shore. When I got there, I thought, *Which way do I go?* I headed to the left and walked and walked, scanning the crowd for my family, but I couldn't find them. So I turned to the right and retraced my steps, searching and searching for my family. Finally, in the distance, I saw that red umbrella. And can I tell you, as a little girl, that was a happy moment for me. I was finally calm and at peace, knowing where my family was and that I could make my way to them. I ran across the hot sand, flopped down under the umbrella, and decided that I was not going to do that again. Of course, I did tell them all about my adventure.

I hadn't meant to lose my way. I hadn't realized that, after playing in the water for a while, oblivious to everything around me, the current had caused me to slowly drift down the beach. The current was imperceptible to me. I was so busy playing in the water that I hadn't even realized what was happening. I was so preoccupied that I hadn't looked up to check in with my family or to stay in line with that red umbrella.

That's what happens in life sometimes. There are undercurrents in our life trying to drag us off course from where we are supposed to be. They could be anger, bad attitudes, not forgiving others, or distractions, but they all have the same result—they lead us away from where God wants us to go.

I can't even count the number of times I've heard people say, "I was raised in church, so I don't know how I ended up so far away from God. I slowly drifted away from what I knew."

The other day, a woman was telling me how happy her marriage was in the early years, but then she and her husband began to argue. She said, "Now we've drifted apart and fight all the time. We don't see eye to eye. Things just aren't the same." Her distance from her husband was a result of the undercurrents that pulled her away from what was truly important.

Undercurrents can get us off course and separate us from the important things God has placed in our lives. They can be so subtle that we don't even realize what's really happening. Those undercurrents can lead us away from the calling God has placed on our life, from our dreams, our goals, even from our family. We don't want to drift from those important things. But if we don't pay attention, that is exactly what happens. God wants us to notice those undercurrents and how they are affecting us so we can deal with them. He wants us to stay aligned with Him.

If I would have made the necessary adjustments throughout the morning to stay in line with the red umbrella, I would have been fine. I would have kept my family in sight and continued adjusting my position so I didn't get pulled off course.

If I had looked up more during that day at the beach, I wouldn't have drifted so far from where I wanted to be. But sometimes when we are caught in the throes of life, we can forget to look up and keep in line with God.

Fighting the Undercurrents

One of the best ways to keep from drifting from God's purposes is to ask yourself questions, tough questions, about what is going on in your life. If you've just had a blowup with your spouse, maybe it's time to ask yourself, "Did I treat them with respect? Did I say something I shouldn't have? Am I honoring God with my choices?" Tough questions help realign and refocus us. We admit our mistakes, we ask for forgiveness, and then we get back

> *We have to be willing to evaluate our choices and make changes to our behavior if we want to stay on the best path.*

on track. We have to be willing to evaluate our choices and make changes to our behavior if we want to stay on the best path. The undercurrents will always be there, but we can resist them if we're aware of which direction they are pulling us.

In Judges 13, an angel declared the coming birth of Samson, who was to become a man of great destiny. God gifted him with supernatural strength to deliver his people from the enemy, but Samson didn't take responsibility for what he had been given, and the undercurrents caused him to drift so far away from what he could have been. He let his guard down, set his eyes on the wrong things, began to rebel against what he knew was right, and as a result he was weakened in his morals.

If Samson had aligned himself with his purpose, looking for his red umbrella, he could have been everything God called him to be. If only he had checked his heart and asked God, "Am I on the right course? Am I walking humbly before you today? Am I using my gifts and talents to honor You?"

Samson could have dealt with the undercurrents in his life by not putting himself in compromising situations but rather by aligning himself with people who had the same values as he did. The Bible states, "Bad company corrupts good character" (1 Cor. 15:33). When you hang around the wrong people, you get yourself going in the wrong direction.

Hanging around the wrong people may not seem like a big deal. But if we don't take care of the small things, they'll become big things. Have you ever said something unkind just to let off some steam? Perhaps you're upset and throw around some harsh words to your family. You may think those are the small things, but they can cause damage to your family and can split relationships.

Have you accepted an invitation to something that you know won't honor God? How we spend our time is important. Sometimes we think the temptations and distractions are just small things. But one look can lead us astray. Don't be like Samson and miss out on all God has planned for you because you didn't realign along the way.

Undercurrents can be bad attitudes or laziness. These are the kinds of things that can cause us to lose good jobs. It's those small things that cause the drift. You show up late for work and think, *Well, my boss isn't here. He never comes until 8:30. Why does he ask me to be here at 8:00?*

After a full day of work, do you go out with friends and miss out on some of the best time with your family? Do you give them your leftovers instead of the best part of the day?

Are you spending money that you don't have and getting yourself into financial difficulty? These are the small things. The Bible calls them "the little foxes that spoil the vines" (Song of Sol. 2:15 NKJV).

Before you know it, you find yourself like me on the sandbar that day, far from shore. It is not a good feeling. You know you've done something wrong. You wish you could just get back to where you started. You run, trying to find the place that you belong. You call out, thinking no one hears you.

However, God can hear you, and He always helps us when we call out for Him. But how much better to live our lives constantly checking in with Him, so that we don't have that moment of panic, when we realize how far we've drifted?

We live in a world that is full of undercurrents; we have to stay on guard. Maybe you've drifted and can identify some areas where you need to do better. It's never too late to get back in line with God. You can still become everything that He created you to be.

> *It's never too late to get back in line with God. You can still become everything that He created you to be.*

When you feel the undercurrents pulling you away from your set point, make the necessary adjustments that you need. Resist temptations and avoid distractions. God wants to help you overcome them. If Samson had done that, he would have avoided so much pain and wouldn't have ended up in the hands of his enemies, blinded and chained. If he had just asked for forgiveness and admitted his mistakes, saying, "Okay, I'm done with that. God, help me to be strong," he could have aligned himself with the victory God had planned for him.

You can start today. It's a new beginning. God's mercies are new every day. If you fall down, you don't have to stay down. You can get back up because of the mercy and the grace of Almighty God. Don't let one mistake fool you. Don't be like the person who eats a bowl of ice cream and then thinks, *Well, I already ate some, so let me just eat the whole gallon.* No, we can always realign. We can push away those temptations. God has given you power inside, but you have to set your mark and go for it.

The apostle Paul says, "Set your minds on things above, not on earthly things" (Col. 3:2). That means to set your mind on higher things, the valuable and important things in life—those things that are going to get you closer to your destiny, and cause you to have good families, strong relationships, and a great job.

Sometimes we go through life not even thinking about what we're doing. We can't live on autopilot. God wants us to be intentional. We have to be on guard of what we are doing and what we are saying.

Most of our day is set by habits, and we may need to change some of those habits. Habits are just that—behaviors that have become routine. We should always challenge those habits. We don't have to get down and discouraged by the bad habits we've developed. Our attitude should be, *I can change this. I don't have to go with the crowd. I don't have to waste my time. I don't have to gossip. I don't have to be ugly to people. I can control myself.* You can say no to the undercurrents that have led you away from your goal. Push against them so you can get back on track.

Hebrews 12 says to lay aside the weights and the sins that can easily entangle you (see v. 1). No matter how many mistakes you've made or where you find yourself today, it's never too late to get back in line with God. God has a purpose and a destiny for you. You are growing and He is working on you. He says you're going from glory to

> *No matter how many mistakes you've made or where you find yourself today, it's never too late to get back in line with God.*

glory. Now do your part, keep Him in your sight, and continue to strive toward the exceptional life God has for you.

God Is Doing a New Thing

We all go through times in our lives that can become all-consuming. Sometimes it can be a difficult situation, like a devastating diagnosis, or a family member's betrayal. It can be hard during those times to remember to ensure you're aligned with God. You have so many other things to think about. But it is exactly in those moments when we most need to look to God.

Many years ago, I faced a situation that left me feeling helpless, defeated, and unable to see the light. It was hard to find the hope and joy in each day. I was drifting, letting the undercurrent pull me away from who God called me to be. One day I felt like God was speaking to my heart and saying, "You cannot live like this. It is time for you to rise and shine. Lift your eyes and look beyond this problem at the new opportunities that I have in your future."

One of the names of God in the Old Testament is Jehovah Nissi. It means "the Lord our banner." One translation says, "The Lord our banner of victory and conquest." A banner is used to remember and commemorate; it identifies you as part of a certain group. Everywhere we go, God has put a banner of victory over our heads. It signifies this truth: "I am a child of the Most High God. I am destined to live in victory. I can do all things through Christ. When the enemy comes against me, I will raise my banner of victory."

I hadn't realized that I was allowing my feelings of defeat to stop me, block my blessings, and steal my purpose. I had to say, "No, I will not put on a cloak of defeat. I will raise my banner of victory." It wasn't easy. I didn't feel victorious every morning. But I continued to wave my banner of victory. I stayed aligned with God and His truth. I fought back against the undercurrents that wanted to lead me astray. I woke up each morning and proclaimed, "This problem cannot keep me from living in God's joy. I serve a great God, and He has amazing things in my future."

Knowing that God had placed this banner of victory over me, I was going to keep moving forward in the right direction so that

God could continue to work in my life. This is what God spoke through the prophet Isaiah: "Forget the former things; do not dwell on the past. See, I am doing a new thing! Now it springs up; do you not perceive it? I am making a way in the wilderness and streams in the wasteland" (Isa. 43:18–19).

Sometimes we can focus in on the wasteland and forget that God is forging new streams. We begin to think that God can work only when we get out of the wilderness. But no, God can work even then. We don't have to wait for our difficult situations to be resolved before God will do a new thing. He is always at work in our lives. When we learn to look up from our problems and the challenges that we face, and keep our eyes on God and how He is making a way, we can move forward in faith and begin to live the exceptional life God has planned for us.

> *We don't have to wait for our difficult situations to be resolved before God will do a new thing. He is always at work in our lives.*

It was during those years, when the situation wasn't resolved, that God showed me amazing things and uncovered gifts and talents in myself that I didn't know I possessed. Ultimately, God vindicated me and resolved the situation that had caused so much stress. By the end of it all, I was stronger than before and more steeped in God's promises. God wasn't waiting for that situation to be resolved to do new things. He was at work even in the midst of my difficulties. If I would have stayed in defeat, I would have missed out on the God-given opportunities He had in store for me during that time.

God doesn't want us to stop living when things get tough but to keep looking for where He is leading us. Several years ago, I was meeting with a woman from our congregation whose husband had

> *God doesn't want us to stop living when things get tough but to keep looking for where He is leading us.*

recently left her. It was a betrayal she hadn't seen coming and she was devastated. As we talked, and cried, and prayed over this situation, after several months, I began to realize something. She was so focused on the chance that she and her husband might reconcile that she couldn't do anything until that happened. Her life was at a complete standstill, a holding pattern, as she waited for her husband to come back. Now, obviously I knew this was what my friend wanted, but it pained me to see her getting stuck as she waited for this prayer to get answered. It was like there could be nothing new in her life until he came back to her. Finally, I told her, "Listen, you can't stop living. Believe, keep praying, but don't wait for this prayer to be answered before you make plans for your life. You're too valuable. You have gifts and talents God wants to use. Don't get stuck. Raise your banner of victory. Look for what God is doing, and keep living."

I read an article recently about eyestrain, which, apparently, is becoming more and more of a problem because of all the time we spend staring at our computer screens, tablets, and smartphones. Eyestrain occurs when you focus on your screen for so long that you get dry eyes, a headache, or blurry vision. The article said that the solution to this is simple. To alleviate eyestrain, you should get up, look out a window, and cast your eyes into the distance, taking in all the life around you: the clouds, the trees, the sky. The article says that it relaxes the lens of your eyes. Studies show that when you look up and out, it is like you set a refresh button for your eyes.

How much better would it be if we incorporated that same principle in our own lives? How much better for our emotions and our outlook if we looked up and away from our troubles to see the goodness of God? My friend couldn't take in all of the life God still had around her because her vision was blurred. She was losing her identity, her value, her purpose; she couldn't see a way out of her problem.

We have to practice stepping away from the situation that troubles us and cast our eyes into the distance so we can widen our lens and see what God has planned. God has more in store for you wherever you are, whatever you're going through. He's doing a new thing, but can you

> *Look beyond the place where you are right now and see the new thing God is doing.*

perceive it? Look beyond the place where you are right now and see the new thing God is doing. It is springing up even now.

Every morning when you get out of bed, put that flag of victory over your head. Remind yourself who you are. Align yourself with God. You don't have to stay awake and toss and turn at night. God is in control. He's fighting your battles. He always causes you to triumph. He hasn't brought you this far to leave you. Keep that flag of victory over your head, not a flag of defeat, a flag of failure, a flag of "it can't ever happen." That's not who you are. Remember your true flag. It is a flag of victory and conquest. When you raise it high, it keeps you aligned with God and in constant pursuit of His truth.

The Power of Look and See

A few years ago, my son was preparing to leave for his freshman year of college. He was planning to room with a good friend from

home, and his mother and I had worked together to ensure that
we packed our U-Haul with all the things our boys might need
in their new dorm room.

Even in my diligence to make sure my son was ready to leave
the nest, I knew I also had some anxiety about releasing him
into the world. I woke up extra early the morning we were to
drive them to college, feeling apprehensive. I wanted to spend
some extra time in prayer to fortify me for the day. I wrote in my
journal the words I felt that the Lord impressed upon my heart:

> *Just watch and see.*

It's only the beginning. Just watch
and see. Behold I am doing new
things. The essentials of faith . . .
trusting in a promise that has been spoken but not seen
YET!!! God is good and I am standing in FAITH!

I texted those words to my friend to encourage her because I
knew she was feeling the same way I was. She immediately replied
with the words from her morning devotional:

Entrust your loved ones to me; release them into My pro-
tective care. They are much safer with Me than in your
clinging hands . . . My Presence will go with them wherever
they go, and I will give them rest. This same Presence stays
with you as you relax and place your trust in Me. Watch
to see what I will do.

We marveled at the message that God was sending to us both:
that He was in control and that He had confirmed in our hearts
that He is faithful. "Watch and see!" became our red umbrella and

the victory banner over our heads those four years our boys were away at college. That phrase became our declaration of faith that kept us encouraged and uplifted and brought joy to our hearts. We would pray those words, *God, you said, Watch and see.* And then we could release our anxiety because we remembered God's promise.

The Bible says we are to wait upon the Lord; it doesn't say that we're to wait for all of our prayers to be answered or for situations to change before we can be happy and keep living. We're to wait expectantly on the Lord with joy and passion right now. Our attitude should be: *God, I may be in a difficult season but that doesn't stop You from working in my life. In the meantime I'm going to fly my flag of victory; I'm going to go through this day in faith, grateful, being a blessing wherever I go.*

Scripture says, "The path of the righteous is like the morning sun, shining ever brighter till the full light of day" (Prov. 4:18). It doesn't say some days are meant to be bright and others dim. It says that even in a dark, difficult season we are to have a joy and passion for life. It's good to ask, "Am I shining brightly today or do I have a black cloud over my head? Am I too focused on a problem that's trying to block my light and steal my joy?"

Jesus prayed that we might have "the full measure" of His joy within us. We must tap into those resources, lift our eyes to God, and let His face shine upon us. God has given us His joy so we can live every day in His strength with Him as our banner of victory. Yes, there will be struggles. Yes, there will be situations out of our control. But we can stay aligned with God, even in those situations, and know that He is at work.

If you are struggling to find joy today, consider what you are focused on. God is asking you, "Do you recognize the new thing I'm doing in your life?"

God didn't say, "I'm going to do a new thing when you get all the problems and messes in your life straightened out." He is saying, "Don't wait to have faith when the situation takes care of itself, because I'm doing some new things right now. Look for it."

It is up to us to perceive the new thing. God asks us to "see." Some Bible translations say "look," "behold," "watch." He's calling us to cultivate our sense of anticipation. Watch and see what the Lord will do.

I believe that God has a word for you today. You need to keep on living. Don't focus on an area of your life that needs to change or on something that's not happening. Don't wait for God to answer all your prayers before you can move forward. God has new things springing up even now.

Don't wait for God to answer all your prayers before you can move forward.

He didn't say that you would never go through the wilderness or the wasteland. He didn't say you'd never wonder, *Why did this happen to me?* But God did say, "You're not going to stay where you are. I can make a way in the wilderness." He can refresh you during the times you feel weary, and He can do the impossible as long as you look up to see it and stay aligned with Him. Don't get so focused on the stresses of life that they blur your vision. Look up from where you are and take in all the life that God has given you. There is more in store beyond where you are right now.

EXCEPTIONAL THOUGHTS

+ I will not allow the undercurrents of life to lead me away from the calling God has placed on my life, from my dreams, from my goals, from my family. To stay in line with God, I will find ways to check in with Him daily and not drift from those important things.

+ I will evaluate my choices and when necessary make changes to my behavior to stay on the best path. I will not put myself in compromising situations that don't honor God, and I won't align myself with people who do not have the same values I have.

+ I will stay on my guard, resist temptations, and avoid distractions. If I fall down, I will get back up because of the mercy and the grace of Almighty God.

+ I will be intentional and set my mind on "things above"—the valuable and important things that are going to get me closer to my destiny, that cause me to have a good family, strong relationships, and a great job.

+ I may be in a difficult time, but God is doing a new thing, even today it is springing up. I will learn to perceive the ways that He is at work in my life.

+ I will cultivate a sense of joyous expectation. I will release my need to control the situation and watch for His purposes to unfold in my life.

SECTION III

Keep Your Memory Box Full

CHAPTER 5

The Power of Remembrance

A few years ago, Joel and I had the chance to travel to Morocco, where two of our dear friends were filming a television series about the Bible. We had a beautiful time watching our friends following God's lead and creating something that would bring His message to the world, and we enjoyed witnessing a part of God's creation that we'd never experienced before. The trip happened to correspond with my birthday, so one night we slipped away from the film set and went to a charming restaurant in town.

After we had enjoyed a delicious meal, my friend pulled a present out of her bag and handed it to me. I knew how busy she had been and couldn't imagine when she had found the time to buy me a gift. I unwrapped the paper carefully to find a beautiful silver box, handcrafted by the local artisans in Morocco. My fingers traced the intricate etchings on the lid as the silver glistened in the glimmering candlelight. I looked up at my friend. "Thank you," I said, so grateful for this precious gift.

She took my hand and said, "Victoria, I want to do something that has long been a tradition in my family." She paused and smiled. "It's a little corny, but I want us to go around the table, and each person put a thought in the box. It could be a prayer or a story of how much you mean to them."

She took the box from my hands and began to share about how special our friendship had become to her and how much she loved me. Then she took her hand and acted as if she were grabbing her words out of thin air as she "placed" them in the box. She closed the lid and passed the box to her husband.

As the box traveled around the table, each person shared something special about me and put their thoughts in the box. I felt my heart swelling with emotion. I was so touched by each memory they shared and encouragement they offered. By the time the box reached Joel and my children, tears were streaming down my face. I felt so loved, so blessed, and so celebrated. When the box came back to me, I held it in my hands and clutched it to my heart. I looked at my friend and said, "This is the dearest gift I have ever received, and the most amazing birthday celebration I could have ever asked for. Thank you so much."

As we said our goodbyes and headed home for the evening, the air of gratefulness was still tangible around me. Now, anything my friend would have gifted me with would have meant something to me. She could have given me a beautiful piece of jewelry and I would have worn it gratefully; however, the gift of encouragement is priceless. It has the ability to build you up and strengthen your soul.

Words have power. When we receive encouragement, we feel emboldened. The word *encourage* comes from the Old French word *encouragier*, which means "make strong." Encouragement literally strengthens us and reminds us of who we truly are. We feel embraced and celebrated and those feelings allow us to accept our true identity, as children of the Most High God.

When we arrived back home, I placed that box full of memories and encouraging thoughts front and center on my desk. One day, a few weeks after our trip, I was feeling discouraged and dwelling on the wrong thoughts, like we all do sometimes. When I stepped into my office, there sat my beautiful box. I walked over to it, picked it up, opened it, and shut my eyes. I began to let those words spoken that night wash over my heart. I relived that night and imagined my family and friends smiling at me. I felt the warm breeze of the Moroccan night. I smelled the delicious aroma of food. But most of all, I remembered those kind, heartfelt, and encouraging words. It changed the atmosphere in my mind and gave me a fresh outlook. Whereas before I was feeling down and discouraged, I was now feeling strengthened, encouraged, and hopeful.

I have returned to that box, over and over, whenever I've needed to feed my faith and confidence and offset negative thoughts that were playing in my mind. Those memories fill my heart with peace, joy, and courage. Scripture prompts us to fix our thoughts on what is true, right, honorable, pure, lovely, and admirable—things of a good report. The right thoughts are empowering. They will cause you to rise above discouragement and limited mind-sets that would try to hold you back.

> *The right thoughts are empowering. They will cause you to rise above discouragement and limited mind-sets that would try to hold you back.*

I encourage you to start a memory box. It may not be a physical memory box like the one I have but you need a place in your heart that you fill with good things and special memories. It might be a note that your child gave you or a kind word that your coworker spoke to you. Perhaps those times when your husband told you that you were beautiful and looked at you with love. Maybe it's a time when you accomplished something you felt was impossible, moments of victory and celebration. They are everywhere, if you look for them. Jesus said, "A good man brings good things out of the good treasure stored up in his heart" (see Matt. 12:35). You need to have good things stockpiled in the memory box of your heart so you can go back and draw strength from that good treasure.

I used to have a hard time receiving compliments. When someone would give me a compliment or say something nice about the message I just gave, in my mind I would immediately brush it off and think they were just trying to be kind. I am sure they were trying to be kind and meant what they said; however, it was difficult for me to put their affirmation in my heart as an encouragement. One day I realized what I was doing, so I made a decision to receive the compliment as if it were coming from God. Now when someone compliments me, I not only receive it but I also say to myself, "Thank You, God. I am going to add that to my memory box."

Every day you have the choice to either store up the good or accumulate the bad. Be aware of what is taking root in your heart. Scripture says to guard your heart with all diligence, for from it flow the springs of life. We don't want to accumulate anything that will pollute the flow of good in our lives for those times when we need it. When you are facing a day where you feel discouraged, downhearted, or overwhelmed, take time to pull out your memory box full of the good, and as you do, it will strengthen your life and put a smile on your face.

Remember the Victories

Research has shown that our minds naturally gravitate toward the negative. We all know how easy it can be to beat ourselves up over any little mistake that we make. I read about a study that revealed that positive and negative memories are handled by different parts of the brain. A negative memory actually takes up more space in the brain because there's more information to process. If we aren't recalling the good memories often enough, the negative ones will have a greater impact in our life. In this article, it cited a simple example. It indicted that we will remember losing $50 more than we will remember gaining $50. The negative effect can have a way of canceling out the positive. We must be committed to keeping our memory box so full of good treasure there is no room for the negative.

One day I was looking at the comments that had been made on one of my social media posts. There were a lot of people who were giving positive feedback. But then I came across one negative comment. It was as though all the good comments disappeared and that one negative voice became the only one I could hear. As I went about my day, I realized that one comment was taking up too much space in my life and I was being pulled in a negative direction. It was distracting me and crowding out my joy. So I decided to go back to all the positive comments and reread them so I could store those positive words in the memory box of my heart. Now I had something to recall that would fill my mind with encouragement instead of discouragement. Isn't it true that one negative comment can wipe out all the good comments if we are not careful?

> *We must be proactive and offset the negatives that we will all face in life. It is a discipline we must practice if we are to remember the good.*

We must be proactive and off-set the negatives that we will all face in life. It is a discipline we must practice if we are to remember the good.

In the Old Testament, God commanded His people to enjoy certain feasts and special times of national celebrations. His purpose was so they would remember what He had done. He gave them detailed instructions on how they were to stop what they were doing several times a year, take some time off, and celebrate how God had always been there for them. They were never to forget how He brought them out of captivity and defeated their enemies. He also instructed them to put down "memorial stones." These were big stones, similar to today's historical markers, that were placed in the midst of their community to remind them of specific miracles and victories, such as when they crossed over the Jordan River on dry ground and entered the Promised Land. These memorial stones constantly refreshed their memories on how God provided for their needs and showcased His faithfulness to future generations.

God did not tell them to memorialize their failings, the times they doubted God or did not trust in His provisions. He wanted them to focus on their victories and how He was their deliverer. The Psalmist said, "I recall the many miracles You have done. They are constantly in my thoughts. I cannot stop thinking about them" (see Ps. 77:11–12). What are you memorializing? What is constantly in your thoughts? When you look back over your life, you shouldn't remember when you failed, when you went through a divorce, when a business went under, or when the boss did you wrong. That's remembering what you're supposed to forget.

Remember when God brought somebody great into your life when you were lonely. Remember when God supernaturally healed you when the medical report said there was no hope. Maybe God gave you a reason to smile when there was a sad time in your life and you didn't think you'd see another happy day. He gave you joy for mourning and a garment of praise for your spirit of heaviness. Remembering the right things will strengthen your faith and help you overcome your difficulties.

When David first saw the giant Goliath, he could have done what every soldier in the Israelite army did—felt overwhelmed by Goliath's size, his threatening accusations, battle experience, and the sharpness of his spear. David could have remembered how his father left him in the fields when Samuel showed up looking for the king. He could have let those memories dominate his heart and defeat his courage, but David didn't let those experiences take up all the space in his life. He didn't make a habit of focusing on the negatives. Rather, Scripture says that David remembered how he had killed a lion and a bear with his own hands (see 1 Sam. 17:37). What gave him strength was remembering his past victories and how God helped him overcome. After a lion and a bear, why not Goliath as well?

If you're going to stay encouraged and bring down what may feel like a giant challenge, you have to remember that lion and bear you killed in the past, those victories when God helped you overcome what you could not face on your own. Those are your memorial stones. Those are your victories. Write them down and read them out loud. Tell them to your family and children. When you do, your faith will be strengthened and no giant will feel too big to conquer.

Remember the Miracles

When I was in the second grade, I became incredibly ill. My parents didn't know what was wrong. They took me to the hospital, where I was admitted for observation. For six weeks, the doctors couldn't figure out why I was sick. I was on so many IVs that my arm ached and was stiff. Finally, they diagnosed me with a form of meningitis. It was a scary time, but having a diagnosis meant they knew how to treat me. After several months, I was able to go back to school. My classmates held a big welcome-back party for me. I had been worried that being out of school for so long would mean that I would have to be held back, but my teachers worked with me so I could make up my work, and I was able to move on to the next grade level with the rest of my class. That victory is in my memory box. I realize it was the goodness of God that spared my life. I don't take for granted the healing and restoration that He showed me. When I think back on it, the fact that God healed me reminds me that I have purpose and destiny. It reminds me that He's taken care of me and will continue to take care of me and my family.

Every one of us has seen God's goodness and favor. He's made ways where it didn't seem possible. He's given us promotions, brought the right people into our lives, and kept us from accident and harm. It was at the forefront of our minds at that time, knowing it was the hand of God, but somehow as time passes, the memory fades. We can't let what was once miraculous become something ordinary. Don't lose the awe of what God has done. Remember the day your child was born, remember when you met that

> *We can't let what was once miraculous become something ordinary.*

person and fell in love, remember when you graduated from college, when God blessed you with that job, or when you were protected from a car accident. Put up memorial stones. Keep your memory box full of what is valuable in your life and go back to it often. Get in the habit of dwelling on the good and remember all that God has done for you.

I never got tired of hearing Joel's father tell the story of how he gave his life to Christ, a story I heard hundreds of times. He was seventeen years old when it happened, but over a half century later he was still telling it like he had just experienced it. He never lost the wonder of it. When you're constantly thinking and talking about God's goodness as he did, reliving His miracles and recounting what He's done, you're opening the door for God to do something even more amazing.

God wants us to remember the good. When we remember the good, it helps us through the tough times.

One day the disciples had just witnessed one of the greatest miracles recorded in Scripture. Jesus took five loaves of bread and two fish and used it to feed over five thousand people. Late in the day, Jesus told the disciples to take the boat and go on ahead of Him to Bethsaida while He sent the people home. Late that night, a big storm arose while they were still in the middle of the lake. The wind blew hard against them, and the waves threatened to capsize the boat. The disciples were struggling at the oars, worried about their safety, when Jesus came walking toward them on the water, terrifying all of them. As He climbed into their boat, the winds stopped and the waves immediately calmed.

Scripture gives us insight into why they were so worried. The Bible says, "They considered not the miracle of the loaves" (Mark 6:52 KJV). Another translation says, "They still didn't understand the significance of the miracle of the loaves." Here, just a few hours earlier, they had watched Jesus miraculously feed a crowd of thousands. When the winds blew and the waves were rough, if they had just considered and remembered the miracle they had participated in earlier that day, and how Jesus had promised that He was going to meet them on the other side of the lake, they could have stayed in peace. They would have understood that He was in control and all would be well.

They let their circumstances cause them to forget the miracles that God had done.

It's easy to let your stormy circumstances—the child who's off course, the possible layoff at work, the parent who's not doing well—cause you to be anxious and feel stressed out. Rather than keep straining at the oars and fighting the waves, why don't you pause and remember what God has done for you in the past? Jesus said you should "consider the miracle of the loaves"—the times when God made a way when you didn't see a way. Recall the times He gave you that sudden good break and you knew that He climbed in your boat. The way you build strength to overcome obstacles and reach new levels is by recalling God's faithfulness. That's what builds our faith and gives us confidence to move forward.

> *The way you build strength to overcome obstacles and reach new levels is by recalling God's faithfulness.*

Remember the Dream

When Joseph was a teenager, God put a dream in his heart that one day he would rule a nation. Rather than keep that dream to himself, Joseph told his older brothers about how he saw their sheaves gathering around his sheaf and bowing down to it. His brothers were already jealous of Joseph because he was their father's favorite, and this latest statement angered them even more. They made plans to kill him by throwing him into a pit with the intention of leaving him there to die. When they saw a caravan of Ishmaelite traders who were on their way to Egypt, the brothers decided to sell Joseph as a slave. Eventually he was purchased by Potiphar, one of Pharaoh's officials.

When they arrived in Egypt, Potiphar put Joseph in charge of his household, and within days everything began to flourish. Potiphar marveled at this until his wife falsely accused Joseph of a crime. Joseph was thrown in prison, where he was kept locked away for years. Even in prison, the warden saw that God was with Joseph, so the warden trusted him and put him in charge of all the other prisoners. Joseph also became known for being able to interpret dreams. One night Pharaoh had a profound dream, but he didn't know what it meant. One of his men told him about Joseph, so Pharaoh brought Joseph out of prison to see if he could interpret the dream. Pharaoh was so impressed with Joseph that he put him in charge of the affairs of the whole nation.

Years later, a great famine struck the land. People living inside and outside of Egypt were threatened with starvation, and because of Joseph's wise planning, Pharaoh owned the only source of food. Joseph's brothers traveled to the palace, hoping to buy provisions for their families. They were met by Joseph, who was in charge of selling the grain. Though Joseph recognized them immediately, they didn't recognize him or realize that it was their younger brother.

Here Joseph was face-to-face with the very brothers who had caused him so much pain. He had suffered for years, unfairly as a slave in prison, before he was finally respected and given a position of honor. Most people would have lived for this moment, a moment where they could finally pay back the ones who had caused them so much misery and heartache.

Scripture says that when Joseph saw his brothers, he remembered his dream (see Gen. 42:9). He remembered the dream that was now coming to pass and how God had been faithful to him. He didn't remember the unfairness and all the injustice, the lost years, and the lonely suffering. He remembered the dream. Joseph stayed in faith. Years later, Joseph would tell his brothers, "You intended to harm me, but God intended it all for good. He brought me to this position so I could save the lives of many" (Gen. 50:20 NLT).

The only way Joseph could keep going through all the difficulties, all the hardships, was by keeping his memory box full of the right things. Believing God had a plan for his life. Don't focus on what hasn't worked out, the disappointments, the delays, the times you weren't treated right. When you remember what God promised you, it keeps you encouraged, it builds your faith, and it helps you move forward and become exceptional.

Faith is all about believing it before you see it; it's about trusting that God is in control when things aren't going your way; it's knowing that what He promised overrides all the forces that are trying to stop you. If we could do it by ourselves, it wouldn't

take faith. You may not see how
your dream could work out, but
God is working behind the scenes.
His favor on your life will take you
where you couldn't go on your own.

> *If we could do it by ourselves, it wouldn't take faith.*

Joseph didn't have any signs that his dream would ever come to pass—everything said just the opposite—but He kept remembering his dream. He could have gone back to negative memories and relived his brothers throwing him into the pit; he could have become discouraged and bitter. Instead he chose to remember what God had put in his heart. He kept his mind filled with promises of hope and faith, knowing that God was still directing his steps even when he didn't understand it. In the times you don't understand and when circumstances seem like they're not going to work out, you may be tempted to relive the disappointments, the hurts, and the unfair situations. Instead push away those thoughts; don't let them take up valuable space in your life. Fill your mind with the good things God has done. In order to keep your dream alive, remember that God has surrounded you with His favor and His blessings are chasing you down. Because you delight yourself in the Lord, He will give you the desires of your heart. Whatever God has put on the inside, no matter how long it's been, no matter how impossible it

> *In order to keep your dream alive, remember that God has surrounded you with His favor and His blessings are chasing you down.*

looks, God can still bring it to pass. He's the giver of all dreams. He's the one who put that desire in you.

Keep recalling your dreams, your accomplishments, the good

things God has done. Continually remind yourself who you are and Whose you are. Let me help you get started. Put these words in the memory box of your heart: *You are a masterpiece. You are beautiful, you are strong, you are smart, you are talented, you are creative, you are chosen, you are approved, and you are exceptional.*

Write down Scripture verses that are filled with the promises of God and what He says about you. Place them where you will see them every day as a physical reminder and a memorial stone of God's truths.

God has filled each of us with dreams that He intends to come to pass; it is up to us to hold on to them, keep our faith firm, and our memory box filled with encouragement. When you keep your mind going in the right direction, filled with thoughts of hope and faith, you will be like Joseph and God will bring you through every challenge and help you become all He has created you to be.

EXCEPTIONAL THOUGHTS

✦ The gift of encouragement is priceless; it has the ability to build me up and strengthen my soul. I will start a memory box today, of things people have said, compliments they have given, words that remind me of who I am as a child of the Most High God. I will return to that box whenever I need to feed my confidence and joy and offset negative thoughts that are playing in my mind.

✦ I will set up memorial stones and remember when God provided for my needs, when I believed and He delivered me, when I took a stand and won the victory. I will use the power of remembrance.

✦ I will not memorialize my failures, my disappointments, nor the times I wasn't treated right. I will not allow them to take up space in my mind. I will fill my mind with encouragement instead of discouragement.

✦ I won't let the miracles that God has worked in my life become ordinary or lose the awe of what He has done. I will remember them frequently and remind myself of the many ways that God has shown me His favor.

✦ I will remind myself that faith is all about believing it before I see it, it's about trusting that God is in control when things aren't going my way, and it's knowing that what He promised overrides all the forces that are trying to stop me.

✦ I will remember the dreams and the promises God has given me. And I will believe that the Giver of my dreams is with me every step of the way.

CHAPTER 6

Encourage Yourself

The other day, I received an email from a young woman who told me about a hardship she'd recently faced. She thought she and her boyfriend were heading in the direction of marriage, but one day he told her that he was moving out of state to take a new job. This news shocked her. She couldn't believe that he could decide to leave without even discussing it with her. She realized that he didn't love her the way she thought he did and that their relationship was not as special to him as it had been to her.

The first few weeks after the breakup, she said, "I tried and tried to make sense of what happened. What did I do wrong? I blamed myself because things didn't work out. I was consumed with these negative thoughts. I became so discouraged that I didn't want to go to work or out with friends. I just wanted to stay home. One evening, I was flipping through the channels and came across your television program. As I began to listen to the message that Joel gave that day, it was as if he was talking to me. I immediately felt encouraged. I began to listen to the messages on your podcast and on YouTube every chance I had. As I heard those words of encouragement, hope rose within me. I became stronger and regained my confidence. I realized I had been so focused on what happened to me that I wasn't paying attention to what was happening inside of me. I was allowing what someone had done to me to define my future. I had been feeling so hurt, so discounted, and so alone, that it was causing me to throw away all the good things in my life. I realized whether that man chose to love me or not, I was still the same. My purpose and value hadn't changed. I started to put into practice the teaching I heard in your ministry. I began to look in the mirror every day and say to myself, 'You are beautiful. You are talented. You are valuable.' As I practiced this, it became easier and easier to believe. I started to appreciate myself and began to like who I saw in the mirror; the fun person I really am and always have been."

Then she closed her email with this: "Every day I say to myself, 'God is going to bring the right person across my path because I'm in the palms of His hands.'"

That young woman made a choice to overcome the discouragement she had been feeling by speaking words of faith to herself. She used her words to build herself up and rewrite the negative narrative in her mind with the truth of who God says she is. As she began to encourage herself, hope rose in her heart, hope that produced faith, which helped her move forward into her future. Disappointments, hurts, and unfair situations will come to all of us, but we can't allow memories of those situations to dominate our lives. To be exceptional, you must pay attention to what your thoughts are creating inside of you. Your thoughts are powerful. They can lift you up or push you down. Your thoughts can create an atmosphere of victory or defeat. This woman chose the right

> *Your thoughts can create an atmosphere of victory or defeat.*

thoughts and spoke the right words over her life, and as a result, she went from a victim mentality to a victor mentality.

In Exodus 6, Moses told the Israelites that God was going to deliver them from the hard labor and oppression they were facing under Pharaoh in the land of Egypt. He was reporting to them that God was going to bring them out of bondage into a place of freedom. Because they were so broken and despondent, they didn't listen to what Moses was saying to them. Scripture says that they were too discouraged to believe. Discouragement can drown out the promises of God. Discouragement can dash our hopes and dreams and keep us from believing that we have a bright future. It can bury our faith and weigh us down. Things don't always turn out the way we would like. Difficulties are a part of life; however, it is up to us to learn how to encourage ourselves with the promises of God. The woman who was shattered from her broken relationship would tell you that although her relationship with that man was not restored, God did restore her faith and joy and she was able to move forward with her life.

Fill Your Tank of Encouragement

David was a great king, a man after God's own heart, who learned the importance of encouraging himself in the Lord. This mighty man of God, who faced great challenges, knew the secret to overcoming. He built himself up by filling his mind with the things of God. He was able to draw strength when he needed it from what was inside of him. David had just suffered the worst defeat of his life, and the men in his army were so disheartened that they threatened to stone him. At his lowest point of discouragement, when he had no one around him to encourage him, David "encouraged and strengthened himself in the Lord his God" (1 Sam. 30:6 AMPC).

It's great when your family and friends are there to encourage you during difficult times, but what happens when no one's there to encourage you? We shouldn't depend on other people to encourage us. Our main source of encouragement should come from within. You can't look to other people to find your encouragement; you have to encourage yourself. I can't even imagine Joel trying to encourage me every time I feel discouraged. If I went to him each time I felt pressured and needed to be cheered up, he'd probably lock himself in a closet and not come out. And I wouldn't blame him. We can't depend on other people to keep us happy.

> *You can't look to other people to find your encouragement; you have to encourage yourself.*

David believed that he was chosen and that he was called by God to do great things. He gave praise to God in his difficulties and filled up his emotional tank by getting into agreement with God. Too often we get out of agreement with God when we make a mistake or when things don't go our way. We are critical about ourselves and we talk negatively about our situations. We find it easy to recognize the good qualities in other people, yet completely ignore our own positive qualities. Instead, we seem to only see what we're doing wrong, or all the times we blow it. We have to remind ourselves that we are not failures; we are learners.

You may be saying, "Victoria, things haven't gone my way. I feel like I have had some major setbacks." Can I remind you of something? You are still here. You are still full of purpose and potential. You still have a bright future. You can't dwell on the things that haven't worked out or what you can't seem to accomplish and still expect to walk in strength and courage. We are all in the process of becoming who God created us to be. It is up to us to stay encouraged along the way. We are made in the image of God, so when we criticize ourselves, we might as well be criticizing the One who made us. When we encourage ourselves, we are saying, "God, thank you that I am fearfully and wonderfully made. I can do all things through Christ who strengthens me. I may not be where I want to be, but I believe that You are leading me in the right direction." That's how we get into agreement with God and celebrate the God who made us.

God is applauding you. He is a good Father. Just like when a child takes his first steps as he learns to walk, a good parent cheers him on. Even though he will fall down, a loving parent doesn't get mad. He knows it is part of the learning process. Maybe you feel as if you have fallen down today, but let me assure you that God is a good Father and He is cheering you on. He is supporting you along the way.

What if we could start observing the good things in ourselves and applauding even the smallest accomplishments? If you tend to be a procrastinator, when you start that next project you've been putting off, applaud yourself even if you don't finish it. When you have a good day and stay on that diet you started, cheer yourself on. When you're attempting to overcome an addiction, celebrate each step along the way. When we applaud ourselves, we're not being boastful, egotistical, or prideful. By cheering ourselves on, we're building confidence and faith in who God called us to be. Don't go around looking for ways you've blown it; applaud

> *Recognize that you are in the process of becoming the person God wants you to be.*

yourself for all the things you've done well. Recognize that you are in the process of becoming the person God wants you to be.

Joel is an amazing encourager. He encourages people all over the world. One of the secrets to his encouragement is that he knows how to encourage himself. He practices finding the best in himself. A while ago Joel was on a book tour in another state, and after we finished an interview with a journalist, we got in our car. Joel sat there for a second and then he said, "I did a great job on that interview. I did everything I knew to do. I said what I knew to say. And I feel good about what I did today. I did the very best I could."

We had a friend with us at the time, and a little later he said to Joel, "You know, when you affirmed yourself after that important interview, it reminded me of how negative I am toward myself. If I had just come out of that interview, I would have been full of doubt and convinced that I didn't say anything right even if I had. When you had the boldness and courage to affirm yourself, it was very freeing for me. It made me realize that I can affirm myself."

If you're going to be exceptional, you must learn to encourage yourself. Get up every day and begin to declare who God says you are. "I am a child of the Most High God. I am loved by God. I am strengthened by God. I am accepted by God and I am full of purpose and destiny." This will change the atmosphere of your life and keep your memory box full of good things. Then you will have treasure stored up in your heart to draw from. As you continue to encourage yourself, you will have the ability to see the best not only in yourself, but also in others.

Your Words Have Power

The other day a woman was telling me about her daughter, whom she loves so much and in whose future she is deeply invested. The people in her daughter's workplace were not recognizing her talents, and she wasn't getting the breaks she deserved. There were other, less talented workers who were stepping up and receiving better opportunities. Her daughter's situation was breaking her heart and she was so frustrated. She went on and on, telling me that if this situation didn't change and opportunities kept passing her by, her daughter's talent would go to waste.

While I empathized with the frustration this mother felt, I also recognized that the picture she was painting of her daughter's life was one of defeat. As I listened, I realized, *This woman is convincing me this is going to happen. She's getting me upset and worried.* I thought, *If she is convincing me, what are those words doing in her daughter's life?*

When she stopped talking, I looked at her and asked her a tough question. "Is that what you want for your daughter?" She looked at me in shock and answered, "Of course not." So I said, "Then quit prophesying her future."

This mother was allowing her fear and her negative words to fuel the scenario of failure. Her perception of the situation was not helping her daughter create a vision of accomplishment and success, but rather one of doubt and defeat. She was using her words to lead her in the wrong direction.

That mother didn't even realize that her words of defeat were diminishing the dream inside of her daughter. Words have the ability to do that in us and in others. Words are powerful. They

> *Words are powerful. They paint pictures of success or failure. We need to be careful how we use them.*

paint pictures of success or failure. We need to be careful how we use them.

I read a story about a young woman who was an aspiring writer. She was editor of her yearbook in high school as well as the editor of her school paper. Her freshman year of college, she earned a spot to participate in a prestigious writing class led by a traveling Harvard professor. She was so excited when she turned in her first paper, anticipating good news. The following week the professor called her into his office and slid the paper over to her with a big F written in bright-red ink. His exact words to her were, "Your writing stinks."

She was devastated as he continued to spew words of doubt. "You should never write again. You will not earn a single dime as a writer." He told her that if she promised to never write again, he would give her a B in his class, allowing her to keep her summa cum laude status. Because of those negative words spoken over her, she let go of her dream. Those negative words were like seeds in her heart that caused her to quit pursuing her passion to write. About fourteen years later, she was on vacation with her family as a big news story was breaking in the town they were visiting. She walked over to the journalists who were covering the story and struck up a conversation with them. She shared her dream of always wanting to be a writer. One journalist spoke up and said to her, "If you love to write, you should be writing. When you decide to write again, please send it to me. Here is my card."

His words ignited her passion and stirred her confidence once again. She finally dared to put pen to paper and found a joy that she had shelved away years ago come roaring back. Within no time, she had completed a draft of a book and mailed it to the writer. Shortly thereafter, she received a call from his agent. Before she knew it, her manuscript became a bestselling novel. Publishing companies were bidding for her work. Today, she has written countless books, including the novelizations of *Romancing the Stone* and *The Jewel of the Nile*.

Despite the negative words spoken to her by that creative writing professor, Catherine Lanigan has been writing bestselling novels for over thirty-five years.

Pilot Your Ship

In the beginning, Scripture says, God *spoke* to the darkness and created light. Then He began to use His *words* to create the world. Words have creative power. Scripture says there is life and death in the power of the tongue. We have the ability to speak life to those we love and help them discover what God has placed on the inside of them. Words can lift us up or push us down. What you say matters and has a profound impact on all those around you.

In the book of James, the writer compares the tongue to the rudder of a big ship. The rudder may be a very small part, but it controls the entire direction of the ship. How the pilot directs the rudder determines where the ship will go. Even with strong winds and raging waters, that small rudder has the power to turn the ship. But who controls the rudder? The pilot.

Maybe you're in a storm today; the winds are raging against you. You will be tempted to complain, blame others, or speak doubt into the situation. Negative words will not steer you out of the storm. I encourage you to pilot your ship with the rudder of faith-filled words. When you resist the temptation to speak negative words, you will direct your life out of the rough waters and set your course for victory.

David prayed, "Set a guard over my mouth, LORD; keep watch over the door of my lips" (Ps. 141:3). Even as David used his words to encourage himself, he was also mindful of his choice of words. David was in a very difficult situation. He was stuck in a cave with enemies all around him. David was saying, "Lord, don't let me send my life in the wrong direction. Keep my tongue from speaking evil." He knew the power of his words.

The pressures of life are real. It's easy to speak out of frustration. We too need to keep a guard over our mouths in times of stress and pressure. We all face difficult times that weigh heavy on us. When I don't know what to say, I just begin to praise God and thank Him. I say, "Father, thank You that You are stronger than anything that is coming against me. God, it may look bad, but You are good. You can do anything but fail me." Then I begin to sing the worship songs that we sing every week in church. I have those songs in my heart so they come out of my mouth. I go back to my memory box so I can praise my way to victory. God has given us the ability to use our words and release our faith so we can pilot our lives through the storms and straight to Jesus.

> *God has given us the ability to use our words and release our faith so we can pilot our lives through the storms and straight to Jesus.*

Go After Your Miracle

Mark 5 tells the story about the woman who had suffered with bleeding in her body for twelve long years. She had been to many doctors and had done everything she could. She spent all of her money trying to find a cure, but she wasn't getting better, only worse. She was frail and weak. One day she found out Jesus was passing through her town, so she went to see Him. I am sure she had heard stories of how he had healed a crippled man, cured another from leprosy, and made blind men see. Something came alive on the inside of her and she thought, *If He did this for other people, He could certainly do this for me*. The streets were crowded and buzzing with people. She could have been thinking, *I'll never be able to make it through all the people in the streets. I am weak and exhausted*. She could have been complaining, saying, "Life isn't fair. Why did this happen to me?" Instead she said to herself, "If I can only get to Jesus and touch the hem of His garment, I know I will be healed." One version says, "She *kept* saying to herself. She repeated it over and over, 'When I get to Jesus, I know I will be well. I know healing is coming. I may be weak and exhausted, but my miracle is on the way.'" It was the words of faith coming out of her mouth that gave her the strength to go after her miracle. She encouraged herself along the way so she could keep going.

The streets were crowded with people, and her body was weak and frail because she had been losing blood for years. Instead of looking at the problem, she began to release faith-filled words that gave her the ability and strength that day to get out of her home and begin to push through the crowd. Most people would have given up, but not this woman. She was determined and had a made-up mind. She found herself in the crowd near Jesus. I can see her now, pushing through and saying to herself, "If I can only get to Him, if I can touch Him." She came up behind Jesus and gave one last, "If I can only get to Him." With her final bit of strength and determination, she stretched out her hand and touched the hem of His robe. Immediately she knew her life was changed.

Jesus looked at His disciples and asked, "Who touched Me?"

They looked at him in confusion and said, "There are many touching you, Lord. Everybody's crowding around us."

Jesus turned around, looked at that woman, and saw her faith. He said, "Woman, you are healed."

Her words led her to her miracle and changed the course of her life. In order to get her miracle, she not only had to fight through the crowd of people that day, she had to fight through the thoughts that could have crowded her mind.

Is your mind crowded with thoughts that are telling you, *You will never meet the right person* or *You will never see your dreams come to pass*? The crowd could be negative words people have spoken over you. *You're not good enough. You don't have the talent you need. You will never be successful.* You may have to fight through the crowd of broken dreams, financial problems, or mistakes you made. The crowd could be telling you to stay home. You have tried everything and it is not going to work out. If you are going to be exceptional, you have to be more determined than the crowd of thoughts that are coming against you.

> *If you are going to be exceptional, you have to be more determined than the crowd of thoughts that are coming against you.*

Jesus is passing by. Expect things to change. Keep encouraging yourself: "My breakthrough is coming. Opportunities are on the way."

Jesus said, "My words are spirit and they are life."

I want to encourage you to take the words of God and speak them audibly out of your mouth. It will change your thoughts and lead you to your miracle.

When that woman said, "If I can only touch Him, I'll be healed," she prophesied her future. The winds or storms may be coming against you, but you can direct your ship with the words you speak. You can pass through those storms and get on the course to your miracle today. Your words can lead you to the very garment of Jesus.

EXCEPTIONAL THOUGHTS

✦ I am responsible to encourage and strengthen myself in the Lord my God and His promises. I cannot depend on my family or friends to encourage me. I will encourage myself and rewrite any negative narrative that comes against me.

✦ I will fill my encouragement tank right now by getting in agreement with what God says about me. I am fearfully and wonderfully made in the image of God. I will accomplish goals and overcome temptations. I will celebrate the fact that I am becoming the person that God has made me to be.

✦ My thoughts have the power of encouragement. Today, I am going to choose thoughts of victory and treasure them up in my heart, so I can draw strength from them in times of discouragement. I know that God is a Good Father who is cheering me on.

✦ Words have creative power. I will be careful to speak words of faith that set my life on a course of victory.

✦ I will set a guard over my mouth and keep watch over my words. I will not speak negative words but words of faith, hope, and love.

✦ Words of faith can lead me straight to Jesus, where I touch the hem of His garment. I am going to fight through the crowd of negative thoughts in my mind and go after my miracle.

SECTION IV

Travel Light

CHAPTER 7

Invest in Your Future

Joel and I do a lot of traveling these days, and a few years back, we had two work-related trips that were scheduled back-to-back. When we arrived home from the first trip, we were only going to be there for about two hours before we had to turn around and head back to the airport. The entire plane ride home, all I could think about was getting my dirty clothes out of my suitcase. Thinking about that week's worth of laundry in my bags, I couldn't face the idea that we were going on another trip that night. As soon as I arrived home, I dumped all those dirty clothes into the hamper and began to put clean clothes in my suitcase. It was the craziest thing, but even though I was tired and anxious on the trip home, as soon as I refreshed my bags with clean clothes, I took on a whole new attitude. I was energized and ready to go on the next trip.

It is the same way in life—if our bags are cluttered with old hurts, regrets, and unforgiveness, we can't look forward to the next thing God is bringing about because we're still bogged down with dirty laundry. Some people never refresh their bags. Their bags are stuffed with who offended them, how they were mistreated, and what didn't work out. All that dirty laundry weighs them down and makes them feel tired and discouraged.

We all have a decision to make as to what we carry with us into each day. What we pack in our bags is either an investment into where we're going or where we have been. Investing in our past means we focus on what didn't work out, on who hurt us, or the mistakes we made. If we are not careful, we find ourselves repeating the refrain of *if only*: "If only I had been raised in a better environment. If only I would have finished college, I could get a better job. If only I would have spent more time with my kids, I wouldn't be dealing with this." Those thoughts are a waste of time and energy and a bad investment in our future. You can't do anything about what happened in the past, but you can do something about right now. When you begin to focus on what you can change instead of what you can't change, you are making the right investment. The past is the past. God didn't create you to carry around a bunch of junk that is going to weigh you down and keep you from the life He has planned for you.

Every day we need to refresh our bags. When you wake up in the morning, clear out the clutter and those things that didn't work out the day before. Forgive the people who hurt you. Forgive your spouse for what they said. Let your children off the hook for not noticing all you do for them. Forgive yourself for the mistakes you made. Let go of the setbacks and disappointments of yesterday and start fresh and new. Where you're going is much more important than where you've been. If you're going to be exceptional, you have to travel light.

I knew a woman who had been divorced for a couple of years,

> *Where you're going is much more important than where you've been.*

and she had been praying fervently that God would bring someone into her life. She eventually met a man she was very excited about. He was kind, successful, had a great job, and loved God. She was so thrilled about the possibilities, but instead of starting fresh, she made the mistake of constantly talking about what she had been through in her first marriage and how her husband had mistreated her. She was carrying around all of her negative baggage from the past into this new relationship. After a while the man told one of her friends that she was so focused on her past and what she had been through that it impeded their ability to make a good connection. He decided to move on and ended their relationship.

That's what happens when you don't refresh your emotional bags—you carry your stinky stuff everywhere you go. You can't drag around negative baggage from the past and expect to have a bright future. No matter what somebody did or how unfair it was, let it go. Don't let it continue to pollute your life.

One time Joel and I were on a plane coming home from a trip when I began to smell an odor. And it was not good. I couldn't figure out what it was. I asked Joel if he could smell it and he said, no, everything seemed fine. It became worse and worse, where I almost couldn't stand it. I finally noticed that Joel had taken off his shoes. Well, it turned out that he had forgotten to pack socks on this trip so he'd been wearing the same pair for two days. When I smelled his socks, I almost passed out. The funny thing is Joel couldn't smell it. That's the way it is in life. We can't always smell the bad attitudes, the bitterness, the resentment, and the self-pity that we carry. The problem is other people can. It drives them away. It keeps us from good relationships; it limits our potential and stops our dreams from coming to pass. Are you carrying around stinky stuff and you don't realize it? Is there something you need to refresh?

We all face unfair situations in life. We experience loss, people hurt us, things don't turn out the way they should have. We have to make a decision to release those things into God's hands. He wants to give you beauty for your ashes. An exchange must take place. Your hurts and pains for God's grace. The comfort, peace, and joy He wants to give you. It's takes great faith to say, "I'm forgiving that person who did me wrong. I am not going to harbor this grudge and forfeit the blessing God has in store for me." It's not worth holding on to feelings that are going to rob you from God's best. A friend may have hurt you deeply; you may have been falsely accused. You may have suffered a loss, but God wants to help you through those experiences. We have to work with God to shake off the hurts and the mistakes and keep a good attitude. That's when God can give you the beauty. Your past doesn't have to determine your future. Where you're going is more important than where you've been.

The apostle Paul said, "One thing I do, forgetting those things which are behind and reaching forward to those things which are ahead" (Phil. 3:13 NKJV). He was saying, "I don't look back at my past mistakes and relive my failures. I don't look back at the people who wronged me or the situations that didn't work out. I don't dwell on the disappointments, the hurts, and the bad breaks. I forget what's behind and I get ready for the new things God wants to do." He understood that you can't go forward while looking backward.

Joel and I used to play racquetball together. It's a fast game that's played with a hollow rubber ball and racquet in a fully enclosed court. The one safety rule to this game is that you never look back because the ball comes off the back wall so fast that it can hit you in the face and cause significant injury. No matter where you are on the court, you have to keep facing forward and play the ball in front of you.

Life is a lot like racquetball. Looking back at your past mistakes and reliving your failures will only cause damage. Dwelling on past hurts and who did you wrong will ruin your relationships, lower your self-esteem, and steal your confidence. To live in the "I wish I had done it different" or "Why did this happen?" will limit your potential and rob you of your passion. You cannot undo your past, but you can do something about your present. You can play the ball that is in front of you, not the ball that's behind you. Do what the apostle Paul did: "Don't look back." God will take what the enemy meant for harm, and use it to your advantage. Reach forward to those things that are ahead of you and take your swing. That's where your success lies.

Shut the Door to the Past

A few years ago, Joel and I were invited to this highly secured government building. To enter the building, we had to go through two sets of double doors about fifteen feet apart. We stood in front of the first set of doors, they opened, and we walked through them to the second set of doors. However, the second set would not open until the first set closed.

As long as you continue to talk about the wrongs that happened to you, reliving the mistakes and failures and feeling sorry for yourself, you are keeping those doors open.

It's time to let the doors of disappointment close behind you so you can step forward into the new things God has in store.

When we hold on to our past, the new set of doors won't open. It's time to let the doors of disappointment close behind you so you can step forward into the new things God has in store.

I once met a man who told me how difficult his life had been growing up. He witnessed his brother's life ending in a tragedy and told me about how his girlfriend had died in the prime of her life. He said, "As a young man, I faced so many negative things and became so bitter that I had suicidal tendencies. I felt as though I couldn't live with what had happened to me. I couldn't get past the past. I couldn't move forward."

"One day," he continued, as the expression on his face brightened, "I woke up and for some reason I began to cry out to God, saying, 'God, help me move past all this bitterness. Help me take hold of what you have in store for me.'"

He had a strong urge to start running. He didn't understand why, but he put on his tennis shoes and went out and began to run. "Every day as I would run," he recalled, "I would imagine myself shutting the door to the dark past and running toward my bright future. With every run, I felt God in front of me, helping me, and urging me forward." As the man continued to run, God began to change his heart and refresh his mind. That's how he practiced closing the door to his past. He said, "As I kept running every day, running farther than I ever had before, I saw how God was coming alongside me, helping me accomplish things I had never thought possible." This attitude spread throughout his life. He went back and finished college; then he enrolled in medical school. Today, he has a successful medical practice with thirty-five employees and his own clinic.

Just as this man was able to overcome his challenges because he called out to God, you too can press past anything that's trying to hold you captive. Whether it's anger, bitterness, or regret, find your way to close the door to the past. God will help you. Maybe you need to quit talking about your past or stop associating with the people who keep bringing it up. God is saying it's time to move forward into the new things He has in store. Nothing that happened in your past has to keep you from the amazing future in front of you. You can make the deci-

> *Nothing that happened in your past has to keep you from the amazing future in front of you.*

sion to shut the door to the hurts, disappointments, and mistakes. It's time to move forward into what God has in store.

Don't Walk with an Emotional Limp

One of my dear friends had to have foot surgery. After the operation, she was instructed to stay off her foot for a month before she could begin physical therapy. After that long month of being stationary, she was excited to start walking again. At her first visit with the physical therapist, the therapist had her walk in a straight line. Then she asked, "Does your foot hurt right now?"

My friend said, "No, not at all." Her therapist looked at her in confusion and said, "If you're not in pain, then why are you limping?"

She hadn't even realized she was walking with a limp, but when her therapist pointed it out to her, she shrugged her shoulders and said, "Well, I guess I'm trying to protect my foot. I don't want to hurt it again or do anything that'll cause me any more pain." Her therapist nodded and said, "I understand you are trying to protect yourself, but I need you to quit limping. If you don't begin to concentrate on walking normally, your foot is not going to heal properly. You don't want to get into the habit of always walking with a limp."

My friend was just trying to avoid more pain, a very natural tendency. Maybe she believed that her injured foot would always be weaker than the other foot because of what it had gone through. But she had to believe it could be strong again, that it could be fully healed, in order to take the steps toward a full recovery.

Sometimes we experience negative things in life, such as a divorce, a difficult childhood, or critical words spoken over us. If we hold on to those memories that cause us pain, we can take on an emotional limp. Those past hurts and pains can hold us back and become a stronghold in our thinking. Wrong thoughts are like seeds that can take root in your mind. Many times we don't even realize that it's those wrong mind-sets that are causing us to walk with an emotional limp. That's why it is so important to fill your memory box with "can do" thoughts.

Scripture says to renew your mind with God's Word and transform your thinking. When you hear those negative voices telling you that you can't rise any higher and it's never going to get any better, be quick to say, "No, thanks, that's not for me. I am going to stockpile good thoughts." Make a decision that you are not going to limp in your thinking, but you're going to become everything God intended you to be. You may have been hurt, but you are well on your way to recovery.

> *You may have been hurt, but you are well on your way to recovery.*

Every Sunday during the prayer time at our church, Joel makes declarations of faith over our congregation. He declares, "You are blessed. You are focused. You are disciplined, talented, and well able to do what God has called you to do." He makes those declarations of faith over us each week. What he is doing is putting into our thinking what God says about us and reminding us who we are and what we are able to do. God's Word works when you put it into your heart and mind. Every day you should make declarations of faith over your own life. You may be going through the healing process today, but know that you don't need to dwell on the injury. Declare over yourself that you are healed, you are blessed, and you are more than a conqueror. God is the healer of all things, and if you will remember the good and step out in faith, He will take you to the place of complete healing so you can live the life of victory.

I have a friend whose young daughter-in-law had just found out that she was pregnant. Her son was thrilled and the whole family was so excited. But a few weeks after their celebration, she had a miscarriage. Her wonderful joy was turned into extreme hurt and pain. She began to question God and to doubt herself. She thought, *Where is God in this? Am I ever going to have a baby? Maybe I can't carry a baby to term.* She told her husband, "I don't want to try again. I can't go there. I'm afraid I can't make it through the pain again." She shrank back in fear and began limping. In the process, she began to withdraw and not act like herself. She wasn't the vibrant young woman she once was. It's easy to be scared to trust when you have been hurt or have faced problems in the past, but you don't have to face them on your own. Hold on to God and embrace His promises. His plans are to prosper you and not to harm you.

> *Hold on to God and embrace His promises. His plans are to prosper you and not to harm you.*

Soon after her great loss, a friend encouraged her to listen to our Sirius XM channel 128. She heard the message of hope found in the faithful, loving God who wanted to help and strengthen her. Day after day she listened, and as she did, those messages of God's love began to break down the pattern of thinking that had formed a stronghold in her mind. Courage and determination began to take root and she began to ask herself, "Can I do this? Am I ready to try again?" With time, the defeat and the doubt turned into hope, faith, and victory. She told her husband, "I want to have a baby. I know that God is good and He loves me. I believe I am ready to try again." She pushed aside all of the fear and doubt and replaced it with faith and expectation. Eventually, she gave birth to a beautiful baby girl she named Mia. She broke through the lies that tried to defeat her and the thoughts that could have caused her to walk with an emotional limp. With God's help, she was able to renew her mind-set, restore her relationship, and grow her beautiful family.

You can't allow a painful experience to trick you into thinking you're going to have a painful life. God can heal your hurts. He is the mender of broken hearts. Today, you can rise up in the strength of Almighty God and say, "I wasn't designed to limp. I was made to run. I will not be held in a stronghold of fear. I will walk confidently forward in the things of God."

He will make you stronger than you have ever been before. Make the choice to walk through the process of recovery. Fill your mind and heart with messages of hope from God's Word. It will build courage and determination and fill you with faith and victory.

We Are on the Winning Team

Several years ago, my nephew started playing football. Because he is a strong, stocky boy, he started practicing with the varsity team as a freshman. When he came home after the first couple of practices, every muscle in his body ached and he was bruised all over. I'm sure he wondered whether the hard work, the pain, and the bruises were worth it, but he went back to practice again and again. Finally, it was the day of his first game and he came home that night, rejoicing over his first victory. "I don't care about the bruises. We won! We won!" My nephew learned a very important lesson. He realized that all those bumps and bruises, although sore and uncomfortable, were building in him strength, character, and endurance. He began to understand that persevering through the difficulties were part of the game. Overcoming the challenges and seeing the victories made it all worth it.

Bumps and bruises are a part of life and come to all of us, but you have to continuously remind yourself that you are on God's team. You're on the winning side. Your attitude should be "These bruises hurt, but they're not stopping me. I know in the end I will have the victory and it will be worth it."

When we work to invest in our future and the victory in front of us, it keeps us going even in those times when we feel disappointment and discouragement. In Scripture, the prophet Samuel had spent a lot of time mentoring King Saul and loving him like one of his own sons. But when Saul continued to disobey God and stray from the path God laid out for him, God rejected Saul as king.

> *When we work to invest in our future and the victory in front of us, it keeps us going even in those times when we feel disappointment and discouragement.*

Samuel was devastated. He had given so much of his time, emotion, and energy to Saul. Scripture says that Samuel "mourned constantly for him." Samuel was nursing a wounded heart. We all go through seasons of loss or heartbreak. It's especially difficult when the wrenching pain you go through is because of someone else's bad choices. But God doesn't want us to let our mourning become excessive. Finally, God said, "Samuel, you have mourned long enough for Saul." He was saying, "Quit mourning over what I've rejected. Stop putting energy into what didn't work out. It's time to move forward."

God told Samuel, "Fill your horn with oil and go to Bethlehem. Find a man there named Jesse, for I have chosen one of his sons to be My king." It was time to stop nursing the wounds, to move past the bumps and bruises and remember the victory that was in store. Whatever you've gone through, it didn't come as a surprise to God. You need to do what Samuel did and "fill your horn with oil." Have a fresh attitude and trust in His goodness. David is waiting in the shepherd's field. What God has in your future is better than you can imagine.

Think of what would have happened if Samuel had given in to the disappointment and not trusted God. He would have missed out on the new thing God was doing. He wouldn't have experienced the joy and privilege of anointing David as the next king of Israel, the greatest king who ever lived.

Don't keep looking back. God has a new and better plan. To be exceptional means that you have filled your horn with oil. Yesterday's mistakes stay in your yesterday. Good things are in your future. Believe it, take hold of it, and watch it come to pass.

EXCEPTIONAL THOUGHTS

- I will no longer look back and obsess over what didn't work out, on who hurt me, or the mistakes I made. I will let the past be the past and fix my gaze forward, looking toward what God has in store.

- I can't do anything about what happened in the past, but I can do something about right now. I will begin to focus on what I can change instead of what I can't change.

- Every morning I will clear out the clutter and the things that didn't work out the day before and start fresh and new. Where I am going is much more important than where I've been.

- I won't allow a painful experience to trick me into thinking I am going to have a painful life. God is the healer of all hurts. I will not limp when I was made to run. I will renew my mind with God's Word and transform my thinking. Every day I will make declarations of faith over my life that remind me of who I am and what I am able to do.

- When I get bumps and bruises, I will remind myself that they are preparing me for the ultimate win, for I am on the winning team.

- During seasons of loss or heartbreak, I will remember that God has new beginnings, new dreams, and new relationships already planned. What God has in my future is better than I can imagine.

CHAPTER 8

Make Every Day Exceptional

Two friends were planning a daylong hiking trip. They were going to walk several miles across various types of terrain, then finish up where they began. The forecast was clear, and they had hiked this trail before. One friend carried a small pack containing water, snacks, and a few Band-Aids. The other friend carried a large, heavy backpack filled with a book on first aid, an entire first aid kit, warm clothes, a rain jacket, and an extra pair of shoes. As you might expect, the hiker with the heavy backpack had to stop on several occasions to relieve herself of the weight, only to have to pick the pack back up again in order to continue on.

God wants us to be prepared, but sometimes we carry around things that we don't really need. The weather was beautiful, and the hiking trip was a relatively short one, yet the one hiker worried about all the little things that could happen, regardless of how improbable they were. She filled her backpack so full that it caused her to struggle and expend extra energy.

This is what worry does to us. It weighs us down and prevents us from enjoying the journey. Scripture says that worry cannot add an inch to your height or a single hour to your life (see Matt.

6:27). Have you ever considered all the things you worried over that never came to pass? Someone once said: "I've been through some terrible things in my life, some of which actually happened."

God doesn't want us to live that way. To become exceptional, you've got to travel light. Put aside the worries and walk forward into each day expecting miracles, finding joy, and believing in God's provision.

Today Is Going to Be a Great Day

Have you heard of the Monday Morning Blues? We all face them sometimes. Many times we get up on Monday morning and immediately begin worrying and dreading the week ahead. We don't realize that all the anxiety is making it worse. In fact, more heart attacks occur on Monday than any other day. Researchers found that "the Monday peak" is really a "first day of the workweek" peak, and it stems from the stress that comes when we head back to the worries of the workweek. Research also shows that Friday is the happiest day of the week. However, Scripture says, "This is the day the LORD has made" (Ps. 118:24 NKJV). We don't have to wait till Friday to enjoy our life. If we have the right perspective, we can enjoy life even on Monday. Every morning, including Mondays, we should decide that today is going to be a good day.

I've been married to Joel for over thirty years, and every morning he makes the declaration, "Today is going to be a great day." It's so important that we set the tone for the day. We have to resist the temptation to start off worried, thinking about what's wrong and all we have to accomplish. Start the day in faith, casting your worries on the Lord, trusting that He's guiding and directing your steps.

I have a friend who goes out on her back porch first thing every morning to watch the sunrise and breathe in God's goodness. She never takes it for granted, and she expresses her gratitude by simply saying, "Thank you, Father, for this day."

Wouldn't it be great if each one of us woke up with that sense of anticipation and gratitude, no matter where we live, and no matter what our window looks out on?

The truth is that we all have a million things to do, and every one of those things can bring worry and stress. Your day will be a lot brighter if you declare that it is going to be a good day, and then begin it with gratitude. Take a few minutes to watch the soft sunlight filter through the trees and enjoy the birds flitting here and there. Pause for a moment. Breathe in the goodness of God. Enjoy the aroma of that freshly brewed coffee and listen to the chatter of your children as they play. This is the day the Lord has made. Don't get so busy and in such a hurry that you miss the beauty of this day.

Win the War on Worry

Throughout the day, worries will arise. We all have lists of things to accomplish and tasks that need to be attended to. But we can't let those lists steal us away from what is truly important. There is a story in Scripture about two sisters who welcomed Jesus into their home. When they heard He and His disciples were on their way, they must have been extremely excited. I'm sure everyone in town knew that Jesus was coming to their house. But then the reality of the situation must have sunk in. There was cleaning to be done, and food to prepare. Jesus was a guest of great honor, and they wanted Him to be comfortable.

Once he arrived, one sister, Martha, was pulled away to the kitchen, focused on all the preparations that still needed to be made to feed Jesus and His disciples. She was running around frantically trying to make everything perfect. She was so busy with her tasks, doing so many different things, that she forgot to stop and enjoy the company that was in her home that day.

Her sister, Mary, however, sat at Jesus' feet. She wasn't going to miss this opportunity to be in His presence. After a while, Martha became frustrated and said, "Lord, don't you care that my sister has left me to do the work by myself? Tell her to help me."

Jesus said to her: "Martha, Martha, why are you so anxious and troubled about so many things?" He not only called her name once, he called it twice. He knew she was so caught up in her to-do list that she was missing the moment in front of her. He wasn't disregarding the things that needed to be done. He was addressing how she was handling her responsibilities.

He said: "Martha, only one thing is needed. Mary has chosen what is better, and it will not be taken away from her." He was saying, "All the concerns, the crises, the things that are causing you stress, bring to My feet. Stay in My presence, allow Me to fill you." That's the better way to handle worry and stress.

The word *worry* comes from an old English word from the 1500s that means "to strangle." Worry and stress literally choke the fun out of life. It can take precious moments that we should be enjoying and cause us to overlook them. Martha was so upset and so pressured that she blamed her sister and wanted her to worry as well. Worry not only steals your joy but it changes your disposition, strains your relationship, affects your attitude, and soon you're spreading your struggles to others.

Paul said in Philippians 4, "Do not be anxious about anything, but in everything by prayer and supplication, giving thanks to God, let your request be made known" (see v. 6). God knows that there will be times we feel overwhelmed. Paul didn't just say, "Don't be anxious." He told us how to win the war on worry. He said, "Pray about everything." Instead of worrying, pray, ask God to help you. Take your worry list and make it your prayer list. Talk to God about everything that concerns you. That's what prayer is. He wants to help us through life, but He's waiting for us to come to Him. Don't be like Martha, so busy and stressed. Slow down and invite Him into your situation. Thank Him that He's working, thank Him that He's fighting your battles, thank Him that He's bigger than what you're facing. When you welcome Him into the middle of your challenges, you'll have strength that you didn't have, peace when you could be upset, and faith to enjoy each moment.

> *Talk to God about everything that concerns you. That's what prayer is. He wants to help us through life, but He's waiting for us to come to Him.*

Enjoying Every Moment

You may be thinking, *That's all well and good, but I can't just spend all my days sitting at the feet of Jesus. There are meals to make and errands to run. I have clients to meet and presentations that are due. How can I get it all done?* We all want to be Mary, but we have

Martha responsibilities. God knows there are errands to run and challenging work schedules. But we can bring our Mary heart into our Martha tasks. The struggles Martha faced had nothing to do with her to-do list, and everything to do with her attitude about that to-do list. God wants us to bring Him in to every moment of our lives, and when He's there, we will have peace in His presence and our worry will turn into worship.

God created us to enjoy our days and to live them to the fullest. He doesn't want us caught up in worries, and He doesn't want us rushing through the week to get to the weekends. Sometimes I find myself hurrying through things so I can get to my favorite parts of the day. Whether I am rushing through a meeting so I can get to my lunch date with Joel or waiting for a phone call to end so that I can get outside on a beautiful day, God doesn't want me—or any of us—to live that way. *Let me get the kids out of the house so I can have some peace and quiet. Just as soon as the dishes are done, it's time to kick back with a movie.* Scripture says, in Ecclesiastes 9, to give yourself to what you're doing (see v. 10). God means for you to find joy in your work, joy with your kids in the house, and joy doing the dishes as well as watching the movie that follows. It's all in how you look at those tasks and responsibilities that can start to feel like a burden. He wants us to live each moment of our lives as if we were still sitting at His feet, like Mary.

Brother Lawrence, who lived several hundred years ago, wrote a book called *The Practice of the Presence of God.* You'd think, from the title, that the book would be all about prayer, the practice of fasting and worshiping God. Instead, he talks about the work he did in the monastery where he lived. For fifty years, he washed dishes and repaired the sandals and shoes of those living in the monastery. That was his daily work. There is nothing necessarily holy about doing dishes and fixing shoes. But Brother Lawrence knew that this was a part of his commitment to God, to help the monastery run smoothly. He could rush through those tasks, eager to get to prayer time. Or he could find a way to honor and worship God in the tasks that took up most of his day. He soon found that there was no difference between his time of prayer and worship, and cleaning those dirty dishes.

Everything you do in service to God can be a moment of devotion. It is all about the motivation behind your actions. You wash the dishes as if you were washing them

> *Everything you do in service to God can be a moment of devotion.*

for God. You mow the lawn as if you were doing it for God. You go grocery shopping as if it was an offering for God. When you put your everyday tasks into the hands of God, and use them to honor Him, you make every day, and every moment, exceptional.

If you change your approach to things that cause you stress, and shift your perspective, you can bring joy into any task. I have a friend who has a long commute that fluctuates depending on traffic, and she has learned to turn something that used to cause her anxiety into something that brings her joy by listening to sermons or podcasts that improve her spirit. Now she looks forward to that time in the car because she knows it is going to build her up and prepare her for the day. I'm sure there are days when the traffic is particularly slow where worry and frustration try to come, but because she has already dedicated that time to God, she can cast those worries at His feet and bring peace and joy back into the moment.

Like her, you can decide to enjoy every part of your life—not just the weekends, not just the vacations, not just when you don't have any problems. You can make each moment an offering to God.

Release the Weight of Worry

I worked with a woman who had a son in the military overseas. He was a marine, and his troop was assigned to go through the small towns of Afghanistan and weed out the terrorist forces. They would enter homes not knowing what or who was on the other side of the door. It was very dangerous. More than once they encountered explosive devices and other traps that were meant for their harm. As you can imagine, this mother was very concerned. All she could do was think about his safety. She was tempted to worry, live in fear, and spend her time on edge thinking about what could happen. In one sense, she had a good reason to worry. There's nothing more important to us than our children's well-being.

I noticed how this began to weigh her down. She was normally so happy and upbeat, but now she was solemn and discouraged. The worry began to strangle her passion and joy. I shared with her how Scripture tells us to handle worry and stress. It says, "Cast your burden on the LORD [releasing the weight of it] and He will sustain you" (Ps. 55:22 AMPC). Too often we're carrying the burden, waiting for God to take it from us. But God is waiting for us to release it to Him. It's an act of faith to say, "God, I'm turning this over to You. I know You're in control. You have my son in the palm of Your hand."

> It takes the same amount of energy to worry as it does to believe.

It takes the same amount of energy to worry as it does to believe. Don't let your mind dwell on the negative. You may have a good reason to worry, but worry is not only strangling your joy and peace, it limits what God will do. When you believe angels go to work; when you believe negative situations will turn around; when you believe dreams come to pass.

I encouraged her to make a list of Scriptures on protection and safety, and all through the day when those negative thoughts would arise, instead of worrying and getting depressed, she could read over the Scriptures. She began to thank God for His promises. "God, no weapon formed against my son will prosper. You have given Your angels charge over him. You said when the enemy comes against him one way, You would defeat them and cause them to flee seven ways. You promised the number of my children's days You will fulfill." She took her worries, and instead of giving them life, she turned to God and she proclaimed His truth. She turned her worries into worship.

Little by little, she began to commit to this practice. I noticed her demeanor change. She got her joy back, and I could see the smile on her face. Her situation didn't change, but she changed how she was handling it. By the grace of God, six years later her son returned home safely, and today he has a successful career and is doing great things.

Like my friend, you may have a good reason to worry, but don't take the bait. Don't let it strangle you. Don't let the negative play over and over in your mind. Let what God said fill your thoughts. When you do, you'll not only feel the heaviness lift off of you, but you'll be activating your faith. That's what allows God to do amazing things.

When I feel myself getting anxious and worried, I imagine I'm holding a helium balloon. I put all my cares, fears, worries, and frustrations in that balloon. Then in my mind, I let go of the string and release that balloon. As it goes up in the air I see my concerns going up to God. That's what the Psalmist said; I'm releasing the weight, casting my cares on Him. As it floats up I say, "Lord, thank You that You're taking care of what concerns me. I know You're bigger than what I'm facing. Father, I trust You."

Now, sometimes I have a bouquet of balloons, and that's okay too. I release them one by one. God doesn't want us to hold on to our worries. He says, "I want to be part of everything that concerns you." Something happens when I imagine that balloon floating up into the immense sky. It reminds me that my problems are small in comparison to how big my God is.

Keep the Right Perspective

Whatever you may be struggling with today, the worries that are consuming your attention and stealing your joy, leave them at the feet of Jesus. Don't take on the attitude of Martha, fretting over things that, when you look back on them, won't seem that important. Keep the right perspective. Unlike my friend with her son overseas, sometimes we're worrying about small things. When we put them in the right perspective, we realize they're not worth worrying about.

I heard about a college student who wrote her parents a letter that read:

Dear Mom and Dad,
    There was a fire in my dormitory and from the smoke I inhaled, I developed a lung disease. At the hospital, I met a janitor and we fell in love. Our baby is on the way. After

my husband gets off probation next month, I'm planning to drop out of college and we're moving to Alaska.

Hope you're well,

Your loving daughter

P.S. None of this is true, but I did fail chemistry.

Is what you're worrying about worth it? In five years is it going to matter? Don't let the little things steal your joy and weigh you down. Today is a gift. Everything may not be perfect, but don't miss the beauty of this moment because you're worried about what could happen.

> *Everything may not be perfect, but don't miss the beauty of this moment because you're worried about what could happen.*

One time Joel and I received notice that the city was going to put speed bumps on the street where we lived. There were a lot of young children on our street, and often cars would cut through the neighborhood driving very fast. Several other streets in the subdivision already had them installed, and when they did, the city also put up big yellow signs warning the drivers that there were speed bumps up ahead. One day, when Joel was out running, he noticed that they always put the signs in front of the second house from the corner. Now, we lived in the second house from the corner. And these were big, permanent signs. Joel became so worried that these ugly signs were going to be installed right in front of our house. So he went to the other houses and he measured how far they were from the corner. From his calculations, the signs would go right by our driveway. For months, he worried about how bad those signs were going to look. He tried to think of ways to block the view from our house. He even planted a large bush a few feet from where he expected the sign to be. Two years later, they put the speed bumps in. But when they came to put up the sign, instead of placing it in front of our house like the others, they put it four houses down on the other side of the street.

Joel spent two years worrying about something that never even happened. As long as your mind is on tomorrow, thinking of all the what-ifs, trying to figure out how it's going to work out, you're going to miss the joy of today. Are you worried about something that hasn't happened? Are you trying to fix a problem that may not ever be a problem? Don't miss today by worrying about tomorrow. If what concerns you *does* come to pass, you can be assured it's not a surprise to God. He'll give you the grace to handle it. But you don't have grace for tomorrow today. When tomorrow comes, you'll have grace for that day, and the next and the next. God's mercy is new every morning.

Live this day in faith, trusting that God's in control. He knows what you need. Scripture says that a sparrow doesn't fall to the ground without our Heavenly Father knowing about it (see Matt. 10:29). How much more does He care about you? He made you in His own image. He knows what you're facing, the challenges, the concerns. He sees the situation in your health. He knows what's going on with your children. The good news is He already has the solution. Stay in peace. God's watching after you.

Maybe you need to release some balloons, cast those worries that are weighing you down. Shift your perspective and stop carrying the problems that might never come. Get up each morning and make the declaration, "Today is going to be a good day." When you put this into practice, you'll live the exceptional life that belongs to you.

---- ❧ ----

EXCEPTIONAL THOUGHTS

✦ Today is a gift that I will enjoy. I will live prepared, and will not be weighed down with worries that steal the joy from the journey of this day.

✦ I will approach today with an attitude of anticipation and gratitude. I will not get so caught up in my to-do list that I miss the beauty of today.

✦ I will not wait until Fridays to enjoy my life. Every day "is the day the Lord has made," and I set the tone for every day by declaring in faith, "Today is going to be a great day."

✦ I will bring all the concerns, the crises, and the things that are causing me stress to Jesus and leave them with Him. In His presence I will receive the fullness of peace and joy. I will turn my worry into worship and my worry list into my prayer list.

✦ I will not worry about something that hasn't happened or try to fix a problem that may not ever be a problem. I will have the grace to handle whatever comes my way when I need it.

✦ I will not live rushing through things I don't enjoy so I can get to what I do enjoy. I will look for ways to find joy in everything I do and live my days to the fullest.

✦ I will make every day and every moment exceptional by putting my everyday tasks into the hands of God, doing them in service to Him, and turning them into moments of devotion.

SECTION V

Love Well

CHAPTER 9

Better Together

My mother is one of the most encouraging people I know. I saw her sincerely encourage people every day as I grew up. Through her example, she taught my brother and me to not only look for the best in people, but also make deposits of encouragement into their lives. She was good at using her words to build people up and impart a blessing. She always told me, "Victoria, there is something special about every person you meet. You just need to take the time to look for it and tell them."

The something special didn't need to be huge. It could be a sparkle in someone's eyes, or the brightness of their smile, or a job well done on a simple task. She knows that even a simple compliment holds great power. It can help someone get through the day. Make it a habit to find that one good thing in the people in your life.

One of my friends heard me sharing about how my mother taught me to find ways to compliment others. She decided to model this practice for her eight-year-old daughter, hoping she would find small yet powerful ways to encourage people every day. Soon thereafter, she introduced her daughter to a woman at the church. Her daughter said "hello" quietly and politely. And then, a second later, she said, "I like your fingernails." That little girl was a quick learner. You are never too young or too old to encourage someone and make his or her day a little brighter.

Spread your words of encouragement widely. Your words can literally put someone back on their feet. Your words hold the power to keep them strong and give them confidence.

Scripture says to encourage one another daily, as long as it's called today. Have you encouraged someone today? When God says to encourage one another daily, there is an exchange that takes place. Not only will you give encouragement but also that encouragement will come back to you. When we become encouragers, we cause others to rise higher and our lives go to new levels too.

> *We hold the power to lift each other up, every day, to remind each other of the goodness of God.*

We hold the power to lift each other up, every day, to remind each other of the goodness of God. Let's not hold back those life-giving words, but rather look for ways to bring the love of God into the lives of others.

Rise Up

Years before Joel's father died and he became pastor of the church, I would often tell Joel that he was such a disciplined and smart person. I would find ways to compliment his dedication and commitment. I felt the Lord give me particular

Scriptures for Joel when I was reading my Bible. They would seem to jump off the page and I knew they were something that Joel needed to hear. I would write them down and place them in spots where I knew he would find them. He would always thank me and tell me that my assurance and support gave him tremendous confidence and perseverance, but what I didn't realize was the impact that encouragement would have on my own life. Joel tells me to this day that one of the reasons he felt like he could step up and take over when his father passed away was because of all that time I encouraged him and the times I told him what he could do and what he was becoming.

When he stepped up, our family stepped up. When he moved forward, our whole family moved forward. When the water in the harbor rises, all the ships rise. Don't withhold encouragement, because it will always come back to you. The Bible says, "A generous person will prosper; whoever refreshes others will be refreshed" (Prov. 11:25). When we speak encouragement to others, we not only breathe God's love into them, but we also breathe God's love into our own soul.

I think one of the greatest places we can begin to practice this simple truth is in our own home. Tell the people in your life how much they mean to you. Change the atmosphere in your home by encouraging your spouse and your children. It's easy to point out what's wrong. Instead, let's begin to point out what is right, and what the other person does well. Bring value into the lives of those around you by catching them doing things right. Anyone can see what's wrong. People will not always live up to our expectations. We all have shortcomings. Let's be people who are willing to catch people doing what is right.

The other day, I ran into a friend of mine whom I've known for several years. She is a sharp, talented woman who has a strong personality and can be quite opinionated. She was telling me about a recent argument she'd had with her husband. She ended the story with how she set him straight.

As I looked at the smile on her face that seemed to imply she felt a sense of accomplishment, I asked a simple question: "Do you think your husband is a loser?"

She looked at me in shock and immediately said, "No." She went on to explain how he was incredibly successful and was about to be promoted again.

I nodded and said, "Who wins most of the disagreements at home?"

"Me," she said quickly. She had gotten into the habit of pointing out all her husband did wrong, she was making her husband the loser. Quite simply, he was a winner at work, but at home he was always a loser. We want to help our loved ones feel like winners, because that is what they are. We are called to encourage them, cheer them on, and build them up.

We need to be looking for ways that we can be cheerleaders in the lives of our loved ones. Think about cheerleaders on the sidelines of a football game. They don't put down their pom-poms when the other team scores. They don't walk off the field when the team makes mistakes; they cheer harder. The cheer might change, but they don't stop cheering. They know that their words of encouragement can push the team past their mistakes and on toward a winning goal.

We are called to be cheerleaders, encouragers, and to love each other well. This is how we bring about God's blessing in our lives.

You Have a Superpower

You can literally defeat the power of the enemy in the life of someone by your encouragement. The enemy wants to bring feelings of discouragement. He wants to take courage away and subtract from what God is doing. When we encourage one another, our encouragement is a weapon that can defeat the schemes of the enemy. We become like action heroes when we understand the power that encouragement holds. Your positive words and actions can bring healing and wholeness to someone else. Scripture says to encourage one another daily...so that none of you may be hardened in your hearts by sin's deceitfulness. Encouragement can bring light into dark situations and refresh our spirits when we feel tempted to give in to despair.

In Houston, we've had countless floods over the last few years that have been devastating to our community. Many of the staff in the church have had to abandon their homes quickly without warning. They had to leave so fast that they couldn't even take the time to bring anything with them. The floodwaters came swooping in and it was a matter of life or death to get on those rescue boats.

One of our staff members told me about how discouraged she was as they sat in the shelter. She was grateful for their safety but feeling their house was being destroyed along with all of their earthly possessions left her feeling defeated and empty inside.

Several days later they were finally able to get back into their house, it made everything even worse to see that her fears had come true. There was so much damage that they would have to start over. As they picked through the debris, sodden clothing, and destruction, her husband said, "We've got to change our focus and go up to the church to begin to help distribute supplies and help other people." He was trying his best to get the attention off their loss and become a blessing to someone else.

But his wife couldn't even imagine leaving to help others. She said, "I can't, I don't have clean clothes or any makeup or even a hairbrush to pull my hair back. I can't even shower to feel clean." She kept falling deeper and deeper into despair. Nothing was normal; she couldn't believe all that had been taken from her, and she wasn't sure how she was going to make it through this crisis in her life.

And then she heard a familiar voice. She looked up to see some friends whose houses had been spared from the floodwaters. They had come over to see what they could do to help. But they hadn't come empty-handed. Her friend held in her hand a bag of makeup. She had pulled together all the essentials, in just the right shades, to help her friend start to feel like herself again.

That act of encouragement was what this woman needed to take the next step. It's what she needed to move forward and out of this place of despair. That simple act of putting on makeup and pulling back her hair imparted courage and perspective. She said to her husband, "Honey, I guess now I'm ready to go down to the church and help someone else."

Her friend showed up that day as a action hero in her defense. Her friend couldn't change the fact that five feet of water flooded her home, but she could become a part of the healing and restoration in the life of her friend. She imparted courage and bravery into that woman. Sometimes encouragement is as simple as showing up with a mop or a broom or a bag of makeup. Those small acts can make a powerful impact. That is what it means to love well.

Ecclesiastes says it this way: "Two people are better off than one, for they can help each other succeed. If one person falls, the other can reach out and help" (Eccles. 4:9–10 NLT). God isn't just talking about a marriage relationship; He's talking about reaching out to those around you. That is the healthy way to live. That is the way God designed it. We are better together. God has ordained people in your life for you to strengthen as well as people to strengthen you. None of us have gotten where we are by ourselves. We have all been helped, supported, and encouraged along the way.

We are better together. God designed us to be in community. There are times when we feel like it is easier to do things on our own and we don't need any help. People can be difficult and challenging at times. But you won't reach your highest potential by yourself. You've seen how birds fly in formation. They do that because it makes the trip easier. They use 40 percent less energy when they fly together. They could fly by themselves but they understand they go farther with fewer struggles when they are together.

Over thirty times in Scripture we find the phrase *one another*. Love one another. Encourage one another. Serve one another. Comfort one another. You need "one anothers" around you. Don't isolate yourself and think, *Well, I'm strong enough. I'm tough enough. I'm talented enough to be on my own.* You may be for what *you* have in mind but not for what *God* has in mind. He has something bigger, something more rewarding that you can't do by yourself. Are you flying solo? Or do you have a community of faith? People flying with you, watching over you, encouraging you, inspiring you?

I run into people all the time who still talk about my mother and how encouraging she is and how she made them feel. I know people who drop by the jewelry store just to see her so they can get a deposit of encouragement. I want to be like my mom. I want

> *You have something to offer that no one else can give.*

people to feel like I leave them better off than when they came. You have something to offer that no one else can give. Someone needs your encouragement. Someone needs to know that you believe in them and you believe that they can succeed. We can't just obsess over how we can make our lives better. How we can get ahead and succeed. We should always be willing to take time to make someone else's life better. Our attitude should be: Who can I encourage today? Who can I build up?

I walked in the house one day and Joel was sitting on the couch looking at his phone. I sat down quietly for a few minutes while he was texting. After he finished, I asked him what he was doing. He told me he likes to go through the contacts on his phone every now and then, and ask the Lord to put on his heart who needs to be encouraged. "I send them a text, or email, or pick up the phone and give them a call." It was a matter of practice for Joel to look for ways to encourage people.

If you are feeling down today, if you are feeling discouraged, encourage someone else. Push someone else forward. I believe this is the principle of sowing and reaping in action. When you step out to help someone else, you are really helping yourself—you are sowing seeds for happiness in your future.

Strengthen Your Roots

The enemy wants to bring division and discord into your relationships. He will work overtime to keep you upset about what someone said or what they did. The apostle Paul says, "Make every effort to keep the unity of the Spirit through the bond of peace" (Eph. 4:3). It is saying we have to *choose* to keep unity. Look for ways you can draw people closer and love them well. The Bible says blessed are the peacemakers. *Peacemakers* is a compound word. Peace doesn't just come. You have to make peace. Making peace means looking for the ways that you can encourage and bind people together. It's not easy or simple to be in relationships. It takes effort and determination, but it's worth it. And when we live in unity, we have a stronger foundation to withstand the storms of life.

> *Making peace means looking for the ways that you can encourage and bind people together.*

A young woman in our church had been at odds with her mother for over a year. Her mother had given her sister something that she really valued and she felt unappreciated and left out. The young woman was so hurt by the incident that she said some unkind things to her mother and had not spoken to her since. Her mother had reached out to her several times but this young woman always ignored her calls.

One day she confided in me what had been going on. "Victoria," she said indignantly, "I've always had this feeling that my sister is my mother's favorite. And this just seemed to verify that feeling. I can't help being incredibly hurt." She paused and her eyes filled with tears. "But I can't deny that I miss my mother and I know I should forgive her. But I feel like too much has happened and I don't know what to do."

I took that woman's hand and held it in mine. She was battling with her human impulses to nurse that hurt and hold that grudge. She knew she needed to forgive and become a peacemaker. That's why she had pulled me aside to talk.

"If you reach out to your mother and make peace, then peace will come to you," I said quietly. "It may be difficult, but it is simple."

A month later, I saw the young woman again. She came rushing up to talk to me. She had finally gathered the courage to call her mom and tell her that she was sorry for the mean things she said. The phone call went well and she booked a plane ticket to visit her mother. She'd just gotten back and was overjoyed to have rekindled her relationship with her mother when she received an unexpected phone call. It was her aunt. Her mother had been diagnosed with cancer. She hadn't wanted to tell her daughter because they were just getting their relationship back on track. She did not want to burden her with the bad news.

This young woman told me that she already had another trip planned to visit her mother. She had called her mother immediately, prayed with her, knowing she needed all the love and encouragement she could get as she faced this trial.

Over the next two years, this young woman became her mother's encourager and well of support. She talked to her on the phone daily and traveled to see her numerous times. Her mother eventually received the news that they had been praying for: She was in remission. They celebrated together God's healing of her mother's body and their relationship.

Every time I see this young woman, she thanks me for the advice I gave that day. For nudging her to be a peacemaker, instead of a grudge holder, for putting aside a petty disagreement for a renewed relationship that was life-giving to both of them.

We were made to live together, and when we live with the supportive community that God has graced us with, we can face the diagnoses and the tragedies, the storms of life, with more strength because we are not facing them alone.

Did you know that the giant redwood trees in Northern California that grow 350 feet tall and 22 feet wide at the base are supported by roots that descend only 5 to 6 feet into the ground? Now, it seems impossible, given how tall they are, that their roots do not go deeper. But instead of growing deep in the ground, the roots of the redwood trees spread wide. They extend sometimes up to 100 feet out from the tree. They have a broad base of support, not just because of how wide the roots travel but because they grow in groups of trees called *groves*. The roots of these trees intertwine and even fuse with the roots of the other trees. This network of support gives them tremendous strength to withstand high winds and raging floods. Because their roots intertwine, they share nutrition, one tree helping to feed the next, which helps them survive in periods of drought.

> *We were made to live together, and when we live with the supportive community that God has graced us with, we can face the diagnoses and the tragedies, the storms of life, with more strength because we are not facing them alone.*

If we could be as united in our lives as those redwood trees are, I believe we could withstand any of life's storms and droughts. Who are you intertwined with today? Don't destroy your roots. Keep them strong and nourished, so that you may live in unity, in peace, and with the strength and blessings of God.

United We Stand

When you think about that strong network of redwood roots, they are positioned so close together that you cannot tell one set of roots from another. They are touching, no longer separated, but joined together. That's how God calls us to be. He built us to be in community, together, intertwined.

In the Bible, we repeatedly see people bringing each other close to change their lives. Parents bless their children, often through the act of physically placing their hands on them. In Matthew 19, parents brought their children to Jesus to have Him place His hands on them, pray for them, and transfer blessings to them. "Let the children come to me," He said. The bleeding woman who reached out to Jesus in faith was healed by coming close and touching the hem of his cloak.

A hug, a handshake, a high five, these are simple gestures that can take on healing properties that can encourage and bind us together in love.

A hug, a handshake, a high five, these are simple gestures that can take on healing properties that can encourage and bind us together in love.

Touch is the first language that we understand. Before a baby can understand our words, he senses our love through our touch. Research shows that when an infant is embraced and cuddled and hugged, it affects their emotional and physical development in a positive way. That touch provokes feelings of security and safety, allowing them to develop into strong, confident children. When children don't have the touch that they need, their bodies and brains are starved for it, and they don't develop normally.

Doctors know how essential touch is to our early development, and for that reason, when babies are born early and have to spend months in the NICU, in incubators, they make sure the babies are still touched. They often have volunteers come in and hold the babies when their parents are away. Because the nursing staff knows that touch is healing, touch is verifying, touch helps you feel connected to the world around you.

I heard the story about twins who were born prematurely and placed in the NICU, each baby in a different incubator. One of the twins was doing well and growing the way he was supposed to, but the other one was not thriving. The nursing staff began to worry about him, and eventually, one of the nurses suggested that they move the thriving baby into the same incubator as his twin. It would be crowded but those babies were accustomed to sharing space in their mother's womb, so it wouldn't be that different and maybe it would help.

They placed the thriving baby into the incubator with the struggling baby. He nuzzled close to his brother and without any prompting from the nurses, reached out for his brother's hand. That healing touch caused the baby's heart rate to slow down, and his blood pressure returned to normal. Over time he put on weight and began to grow. He was released from the hospital as a healthy baby.

Touch can impart blessing. When the patriarch Isaac was an old man and wanted to transfer a blessing to his son Jacob, he said, "Come close to me." He hugged his son before he blessed him. There is power when you lovingly embrace someone. Don't say, "Well, my kids know I love them." That may be true, but I don't want you to miss out on the blessing. Don't underestimate how much a hug can bring you closer. I'm always reminding Joel to hug our children. I'm a natural hugger and was raised in an affectionate family, so I nudge Joel to keep imparting his blessing on his kids through that touch, even though today they are fully grown. There's a transferable spiritual blessing in that hug. It heals, it connects, and it unites.

I read an article about Tom Herman, the head football coach at the University of Texas. He's famous for working hard to inspire his players and getting deeply involved in their lives. But there's one thing he does before he sends his players out on the field for a game. He gives each player, one by one, a big bear hug. This is not typical behavior for a football coach, a sport that is known for its physical roughness and aggressive spirit. But in an ESPN interview he explained that when he gave them bear hugs, he was letting them know, "I'm proud of you, I believe in you, I can't wait to watch you play."[2] He doesn't always know his players' family backgrounds. Some players say it was the first time they had ever been hugged by a man. But that coach wanted them to feel the blessing of deep, unwavering love. He was saying, "When those guys go out to battle on the field that day, it helps us achieve victory when they know they're accepted and loved."

In fact, Coach Herman says he was raised in the heart of his mother's Italian side of the family. They were a family where even the uncles hugged every time they saw each other. He knows the power of that kind of blessing and the feeling of encouragement, validation, and love it imparts. He wants to pass on that legacy of acceptance, support, and strength into the family of his football team.

Touch not only imparts spiritual blessing, but it also sends a powerful message. It conveys personal acceptance. If I reach out and touch you, it's communicating that there's no barrier between you and me. It brings us into unity. Jesus shocked the disciples when he reached out and touched a leper to heal him. Everyone knew you shouldn't touch lepers. Their disease was contagious, which was why they were sequestered in enclaves outside of town. But Jesus broke down that barrier and

> *Touch not only imparts spiritual blessing, but it also sends a powerful message. It conveys personal acceptance.*

wanted that leper to feel encouraged and accepted. He touched him and then he was healed.

Think of the parable of the prodigal son. The eldest son had taken his inheritance, squandered it, and ended up penniless. When he ultimately decided that it was time to return home, he knew he couldn't expect to be welcomed as a beloved son. He would instead beg for a chance to be a hired servant in his father's house.

What the son didn't know was that his father missed him so much that he would stand outside his home every day, staring at the horizon and hoping his beloved son would return. When that father finally saw his son's silhouette from afar, he picked up his robes and ran to him, throwing his arms around his neck and kissing him with joy. As the son collapsed in his father's embrace, feeling his love and acceptance, all the shame and insecurities the young man was harboring melted away. In his loving and healing touch, his father was proclaiming, "I love you and I forgive you. There is no distance between us. The barrier has been broken. You are my son, and I bless you." I believe that young man never felt the same way about himself. He had his father's blessing. He was welcomed back into unity. He was loved well.

God has designed us to be in community, to love each other, encourage each other, and help each other rise above the difficulties that come our way. You were made to be a part of this system, a network of roots that will keep you strong during the storms and will nourish you during droughts. Be an encourager each and every day and watch your community grow strong, tall, and able to withstand any attack from the enemy.

EXCEPTIONAL THOUGHTS

✦ I will take the time and look for that something special about every person I meet and spread deposits of encouragement to them through simple compliments and kind words.

✦ I will use my words to refresh others. I know my encouragement breathes the love of God in someone else's soul and those same words breathe life into my own soul.

✦ I will change the atmosphere in my home by choosing to love well. I will observe the good things in my family and encourage them. I will cheer them on and keep a positive attitude regardless of what is going on in their life.

✦ I will look for ways to bring the love of God to people. I will use my words and actions to bring healing and wholeness to someone else because my words may be just what they need.

✦ I will not isolate myself and think I am strong enough and talented enough on my own. I will be a part of a community of faith, a supportive community where we love one another, serve one another, and comfort one another. I will intertwine my roots with others and create peace and unity instead of division.

CHAPTER 10

Become a Blessing

Sometimes we get so busy with our own lives that we hardly notice the people around us. We have jobs, families, and a long list of other responsibilities that can keep us so focused on what we need to get done that we forget that God has called us to love well. Not just the people in our family, but also those who God brings across our path who may be hurting. There are people all around you who are discouraged and feel alone. They need someone to bring them hope, show them love, and give them a helping hand. We need to be people who show compassion.

More than ever, this world needs to see and experience the love and goodness of God. If there's one thing our society is lacking today, it's people who will love unconditionally and take time to help. For us to be exceptional, God wants us to be people who are willing to open our hearts of compassion and follow God's divine flow of love.

Scripture says, "If anyone sees his brother in need and yet closes his heart of compassion, how can the love of God be in him?" (See 1 John 3:17.) We each have a heart of compassion, but notice Scripture indicates our heart can be closed or it can be open. We can be aware of others' needs and help them or we can shut

> *The fullness of life comes when we keep our hearts open to how God might want to use us to spread His love and comfort to those around us.*

ourselves off, caught up in our own agenda and not willing to be inconvenienced. One reason we have so much division in our world today is because we have closed off our hearts of compassion. We weren't created to be inward-focused, interested solely on our own needs and dreams. The fullness of life comes when we keep our hearts open to how God might want to use us to spread His love and comfort to those around us.

The Power of a Simple Act

There was a video clip that went viral of a little girl watching an animated movie for the first time. Her mom was recording her watching a movie where a baby dinosaur had fallen down and hurt himself. The little girl was crying because she knew the dinosaur was sad. It was making her sad too. Then she cried, "He wants his mama." She started calling out to that dinosaur. "Call Mama. Call Mama." That little girl knew that mamas can fix everything. In her heart, she wanted to help that dinosaur and encourage him.[3]

She was exhibiting our natural heart of compassion. Compassion is being aware of what somebody else feels, feeling concerned and showing that you care. When your compassionate heart is open and you see somebody in need, you recognize their pain, like that little girl, and you take time to comfort them. When somebody is discouraged, you feel that discouragement and you act to alleviate that feeling in some way. You don't just pass by and say, "God bless you. I hope you get better." You put yourself in their shoes, take time for them, and do what you can to help.

Jesus told a parable about a man who was beaten and robbed and left for dead on the side of the road. A priest walked by, saw the man, and moved to the other side of the road to avoid him. Then a Levite walked by, and he too saw the man, crossed the road, and went on his way. Later a Samaritan was walking along the road, saw the man, had compassion for him. But unlike the others, he stopped to help him. He bandaged his wounds, put him on his donkey, and took him to a place to recover. He took care of him overnight and then gave the innkeeper money and said he would be back later to pay any additional expenses. We're all busy as we go about our daily lives. Even the Samaritan must have been busy. He had to leave to take care of something else, but not before his compassion had been poured out on that wounded man. Jesus' simple words to the people were "go and do likewise."

Jesus did not make the priest an example. He did not make the Levite an example. He made the Samaritan the example for us to follow. He was saying that an open heart of compassion is what we are all called to have. We are called to show mercy to all people, love our neighbor, and keep

> *We are called to show mercy to all people, love our neighbor, and keep our hearts open to the needs all around, no matter how busy we are.*

our hearts open to the needs all around, no matter how busy we are.

You do not need to perform great acts of service. God wants us to be on the lookout for little ways that we can do good.

One blustery cold evening in Chicago, a woman was headed home on the commuter train. Everyone was bundled up in their down jackets and winter boots as they crowded onto the train car. Amid all the commuters, she sat across from an older-looking homeless man. His clothes were ragged and torn, and his tattered shoes barely covered his swollen feet. The backs were so worn down they looked like a pair of slip-on shoes with no protection from the frigid weather. He had on several pairs of socks to try to keep his feet warm but they were threadbare. The train was full of people minding their own business, checking their phones, reading their iPads, waiting to get off at their stop. Across the aisle on the other side of the door, she noticed a nice-looking young man with a suitcase wearing a new pair of black boots that were perfect for the cold Chicago weather.

As the train lurched along, the young man got up and sat down beside the homeless man. To her surprise, he quietly took off his boots and slid them over to the old man. Then he opened his suitcase, where another pair of shoes awaited him. He carefully slipped on those shoes and handed the homeless man an extra pair of socks, saying, "Change into these new socks as soon as possible." Then he zipped up his suitcase. Within a few seconds, the young man proceeded to get off the train at his stop without another word.[4]

He literally gave the shoes off his feet. He didn't ask for any credit, he didn't make a big show of his kindness, but everyone in that train car noticed one young man's act of mercy and compassion.

When your heart of compassion is open, you're constantly looking for opportunities to be good to people.

When your heart of compassion is open, you're constantly looking for opportunities to be good to people. You don't just feel sorry for them. You take action and do something to make their situation better, if you can. When your heart of compassion is closed, you are like the Levite and priest who saw a need and crossed the road to the other side so they would not be inconvenienced.

When you read about the life of Jesus, time and time again it says that when He saw people in need, He was *moved* with compassion. He didn't just feel pity; His compassion led to action. He was moved with compassion and He fed the five thousand. He was moved with compassion and He healed the sick. His compassion was paired with action and produced miracles in the lives of the people who followed Him.

We are called to do the same. To be exceptional, we understand that to love well, we have to feel compassion and allow it to move us into helpful action.

Follow the Love

Our compassion is not just for those moments when we see someone lying on the side of the road. You listen to the inner urgings of love that you feel. Those feelings of love will lead you to an appropriate action that can deeply bless others' lives.

Several years ago, I picked up the phone to call my friend Shannon. When a woman answered the phone, it didn't sound like my friend. I said, "Shannon, is that you?" I heard a muffled reply: "Yes, it's me and I'm going to be okay."

Now I was really confused. This woman sounded upset and she didn't sound like the friend I had planned to call. So this time I used her last name. And the woman said, "Oh, I'm sorry, you must have the wrong number."

Just as I was about to hang up, a feeling came over me: *You need to pray for this girl.* I didn't know who she was, but I felt so strongly that she needed my encouragement. I didn't want to intrude on her business but I followed the compassion I felt toward her and said, "Shannon, I don't know you, but would it be okay if I prayed for you?"

As I waited, I heard the woman begin to weep. She said, "I just lost my father, and I'm so depressed. I don't know what I'm going to do."

I knew that God had put that feeling in my heart for a reason. As I spent the next few minutes praying and encouraging her, I was able to share the truth that she needed to hear: that God cares about her and sees what she's going through, that He's going to give her strength and she's going to see good days ahead. I could tell those words breathed new life into her spirit. She gained her composure, and as we said our goodbyes, she said, "You're my angel. Now I know God still has a plan for me."

There's a reason you feel compassion for people. It's not an accident. It's God sending you a message of how you can do His work. Those feelings are sent from God. He wants you to encourage, to uplift, and to show others His love. In the moment, those feelings may not always make sense. I could have just hung up and thought, *How strange that I called the wrong number, and too bad that she was upset. I'm busy. I have a lot to do.* But I've learned to be sensitive to that flow of love. And because I did, not only was I able to encourage Shannon, but it also blessed me as well. I was so grateful to God for how He was willing to use me to do His work. That's the way God is. When you're good to others, God will always be good to you.

Researchers studied the type of actions that make us feel happiest. You might imagine that things like going on vacation or receiving a generous gift are at the top of the list. However, the number one action that made people feel the happiest was helping other people. When you are good to people and give of your time or your resources, you receive a flood of endorphins that make you feel good. Loving and serving others gives you the greatest sense of happiness. In fact, they called it "the helper's high."

In 2 John 1:6, it says we are to continually walk in love, being guided by love and following love. Notice we are to follow love. When we feel compassion for someone else, that is God telling us to make a difference in their lives. We need to learn to follow those feelings of compassion and act on them, not ignore them. It's easy to think that it won't make a difference or to think *I'm just feeling sorry for someone* and go on about your day. But someone needs what you have to offer. Those feelings are a way that God is speaking to you. He is wanting you to show

> *Compassion is from God and has miracle-working power in it.*

love and goodness to a person. We are called to follow love and let it guide us to right action. Compassion is from God and it has miracle-working power in it.

Often we make following God too complicated. We want Him to speak to us and tell us what to do. We think when He does we'll have goose bumps and the heavens will boom. However, when you're feeling love, you're feeling God.

A few years ago, my friend Jamie, the founder of IT Cosmetics, whom I talked about earlier, kept feeling like she wanted to reach out to that on-air personality who had gotten her the first meeting at QVC. By this time, the woman had retired and was no longer on the air, but she and Jamie had kept in touch through the years. Finally, Jamie decided to call her, to see how

she was doing and to ask if there was anything she could do for
her. The woman was delighted to hear from her but demurred
and said she was doing just fine and was appreciative that Jamie
had reached out.

When Jamie hung up the phone, she still felt this burden, like
there was something God wanted her to do for this woman, a
woman who had followed her own feeling from God, which had
opened such doors of blessing in Jamie's own life. Finally, Jamie
went to talk to her husband about it. He agreed that God was
probably trying to use her in some way to impact this woman's
life.

Jamie spent some time in prayer, and then kept getting this
feeling deep down inside like she needed to write this woman
a check. Jamie didn't know why. It had been many years now
since she had helped Jamie, and she never expected anything in
return. But all these years later, Jamie had been blessed financially
beyond her wildest dreams and she knew that this woman had
listened to God and opened the door to that blessing. Jamie kept
getting this feeling like she was now supposed to be an angel in
her life somehow.

Jamie knew if she just sent the woman a check, she probably
wouldn't accept it, so Jamie asked her to meet for coffee. The
woman agreed, and when she arrived at the coffee shop, Jamie
told her that God had put something on her heart, and she had
something to give to her. But she made the woman promise first
that she would actually accept it. The woman agreed.

When Jamie handed her an envelope, she shared that she
wasn't sure why she was supposed to give her this gift, but she
felt like God was telling her to. When the woman opened the
envelope, she instantly burst into tears.

Though she hadn't wanted to confide her trouble to Jamie over the phone, her husband had been diagnosed with cancer and the treatment was putting a strain on their finances. When she opened the envelope and saw the check, she couldn't believe the way God worked to provide for her. She was so grateful to Jamie and so grateful to God.

Those feelings you get for other people are messages from God. He wants you to reach out. He wants you to act. He wants you to love. So when you think about a family member or friend who you haven't seen in a while and you feel this tenderness toward them, don't let that feeling pass you by. Take a minute to send them a word of encouragement and let them know you care. You don't have to write a check, like Jamie did, but even reaching out can be an answer to prayer.

I remember one morning Joel woke up and had such a concern for a friend he grew up with. They went to school and played sports together, but it had been fifteen years since they had been in communication. All through the day he kept thinking about him, hoping he was doing okay. Finally, I told Joel, "You need to call him." Well, Joel didn't have his number but it just took a few phone calls before he did. When his friend picked up the phone, Joel said, "I've been thinking about you all day. How are you?" The phone went silent. He didn't say a word. After a few seconds, Joel could hear him weeping. Finally, his friend told Joel how his wife had just left him. He had never felt so devastated. He said, "I'm not a religious person, but this morning I prayed: 'God, if You're there, show me some kind of sign.'"

God knows who needs to be encouraged, who is hurting, and who feels as if they can't go on. He wants to use you to show

> *God knows who needs to be encouraged, who is hurting, and who feels as if they can't go on. He wants to use you to show them His love.*

them His love. Follow compassion. Be quick to recognize that divine flow of love wherever it leads. Don't put it off. You may be the answer to someone's prayer. One phone call can have a tremendous impact in someone's life. You may not realize what it means to someone in need to hear the words *I love you. I believe in you. I will be praying for you.*

Be on the Lookout

Everywhere we go, we should be on the lookout for ways we can be a blessing. God puts people in our path. He gives us opportunities to be good to them. It doesn't have to be something big that costs a lot of money. Buy a cup of coffee for your friend, stay late and help a colleague finish the project. Clean the kitchen to give your spouse a night off, take time to give a compliment to brighten somebody's day. Those small acts cost very little. Scripture says, "As we have opportunity, let us do good to all people" (Gal. 6:10). Don't miss opportunities to be a blessing. If you hear a coworker talking about how they have to take their car into the shop, consider offering a ride to work the next morning. You're on the lookout for ways you can help. You notice your son's teammate's baseball shoes are worn out. Tell that person, "Let's go up to the store after practice. I want to buy you some new cleats." Maybe you hear your friends who have a new baby talking about how tired they are, how they haven't slept much. Don't say, "Oh yeah, I remember those days. That's really hard." Be sensitive—that's an opportunity to be a blessing. You could say, "How about my spouse and I come over one evening. We'll babysit and you guys go out to dinner and have some fun." Open your heart of compassion and look for ways that you can be good to people.

Sometimes it's as simple as listening to someone. In Scripture, two blind men heard that Jesus was passing by and cried out, "Have mercy on us, O Lord, Son of David." Jesus stopped and called them to come to Him. They couldn't see Him, but they could sense His compassion. He said, "What do you want?" Now, to some, that seemed like an odd question. Jesus knew what they wanted. It was obvious they couldn't see. But Jesus wanted to take the time to listen to them, to make them feel important. He wanted to show His concern.

It's nice to have someone come alongside you and listen to how you're feeling, rather than just trying to solve the problem for you. Jesus could have easily just touched them and said, "All right, you're healed. Go on your way." But He knew the power of a listening ear. He wanted to hear what they had to say. After He listened to them, the Bible says that He was so full of compassion that He touched their eyes and they were instantly healed.

I've found that many times if I'm just willing to listen to people, it can help start the healing process for them. When people have a lot of wounds and pain bottled up inside, they need a way to get it out. Some people don't have anybody they believe cares about them or they've been hurt so badly that they struggle to trust anyone. If you will step up and show them a heart of compassion and be their friend by providing a listening ear, you can help them get the heavy load off their chest. It's not about being a counselor or having all the answers to their questions. Just be willing to listen. Take time to show you're concerned for them.

A while back somebody came up to me after a service and told me about a situation they were struggling with. The person was talking very fast and kept going on and on. I wanted to jump in and give them some advice, and I tried a few times, but I couldn't get a word into the heavy flow of words full of emotion coming my way. Then it dawned on me: *This is like when I'm telling Joel something big that is bothering me, and I won't let him get a word in because I'm really just wanting to talk it out. I don't necessarily want his advice as much as I just want him to listen.* It was the same way with this person. When they finally finished, they said, "Thank you, Victoria. I can't tell you how good it feels to have talked this through. Now I think I know what to do." Then they smiled and walked away. They didn't need my advice. They just needed to be heard. And that was the start of their healing.

We all have an assignment from God and a ministry we are called to. It may not be to get up in front of people, it may not be to go overseas and be a missionary, but we all have a call to be good to people. That's one of the best witnesses we could ever have. You don't have to preach to people; you don't have to argue doctrine or try to convince them to believe what you believe. All you have to do is be good to them. Your actions speak louder than your words. I can say "I love you" all day long, but true love is seen in what we do. If I really love you, I'll take time to encourage you. If I really care about you, I'll give you a ride even though I have to get up earlier to do so. God said to Abraham, "I will bless you…and you will be a blessing" (Gen. 12:2). One key to being blessed is you have to be willing to be a blessing. God won't increase you in the way He wants if you don't make it a priority to be good to people.

We should have a goal every day of doing at least one good

thing for somebody else. Don't wait for a special occasion. It doesn't have to be Christmas, their birthday, Valentine's Day. Just an ordinary day, bring flowers home to your wife. You're at the mall and you see a blouse that would look good on your friend; buy it and give it to her. "What's this for? It's not Christmas. It's not my birthday." No, it's just because you're my friend and I want to be good to you. You can't be good to everyone, but you can be good to

> *You can't be good to everyone, but you can be good to the people God puts in your life.*

the people God puts in your life. You need to study them, listen to what they're saying. Be sensitive to their needs.

A young entrepreneur was in Africa touring local villages and schools with a group of friends. He was watching some young boys out playing soccer in a field when one of the boys kicked the ball to him. He was thrilled to join in and enjoyed a lively game. As they were leaving the village, the boy who kicked the ball to him followed along, chatting with him in English. The young man couldn't believe how well the boy could converse given what a rural and secluded part of the country they were in. He found out the boy was so eager for an education, he walked five hours each day just to attend this school.

He was so impressed he handed the young boy his business card and $30. "Go get yourself a good jacket, and if you ever need any help with your education, give me a call. I'd be happy to support you."

The boy's face lit up with amazement. He couldn't believe the man's kindness.

Several months later, the boy sent an email. "My parents have given me permission to continue my education. I hope you remember me."

The very fact that the entrepreneur had received this email confirmed what he saw in the boy, a passion and commitment to learn. How had the boy found a computer on which to email him? He couldn't imagine how far that young boy had to travel and who he would have had to ask in order to send this simple message.

It turned out he had walked twelve hours to send the email.

The man was delighted to connect the boy with a friend he had in the capital of Ethiopia. Perhaps his friend could look into schools for this boy. If he found one, he was committed to paying for his living expenses, schooling, and supplies.

A year later, the entrepreneur traveled back to Ethiopia, where this boy was now living with his friend and attending school. The boy was just as joyful and thankful as ever. He had big dreams. He wanted to travel to the United States and go to college. He wanted to be an entrepreneur just like the man he met on the soccer field who was so kind to support him.

The entrepreneur promised that he would fulfill his promise. He would support this boy's education.

What the boy didn't realize was that man was Blake Mycoskie, the founder of TOMS Shoes.

Blake had built his career off his heart of compassion, founding TOMS when he saw the need for shoes in developing countries, how children wouldn't go to school because they didn't have shoes to protect their feet on the long journey. For every pair of shoes TOMS sells, they send a pair to a child in need. To date, they have distributed over 60 million pairs of shoes, impacting so many lives, including this young man's, who is now attending a prestigious university in the United States.[5]

To be on the lookout doesn't mean you have to do big things

all at once, but follow the small steps of compassion that God puts in your heart. Those small steps can lead you on a journey that truly changes hearts and transforms lives, including your own.

> *To be on the lookout doesn't mean you have to do big things all at once, but follow the small steps of compassion that God puts in your heart.*

Every opportunity you have, be good to people. You may not know why God has put them in your path, but you can be assured it's not a coincidence. God is strategically placing people in your life and trusting you to show them His love. Now it's time to do your part. To be exceptional means you understand God's call on your life. Love well. Don't miss any opportunity to be a blessing, whether it is sharing a pair of shoes, buying somebody's dinner, or speaking words of encouragement to a stranger. Keep your heart of compassion open. Follow that flow of love. Not only will you be a blessing, but you will also be blessed.

EXCEPTIONAL THOUGHTS

✦ God's call on my life is to show love, have mercy, and be a blessing everywhere I go. As I give to others, God will bless me in return.

✦ I will look for opportunities to be good to people. I will not just feel sorry for them and pass them by. I will be moved with compassion to take action and make their situation better.

✦ Compassion is from God and has miracle-working power in it. I will remember that one phone call, one word of encouragement, one simple act of kindness can turn another person's life around.

✦ God knows who is hurting and needs to be lifted. I will be sensitive to the needs of those around me. Taking time to listen with a compassionate ear, give a compliment, or buy a cup of coffee in order to brighten someone's day. As I show simple acts of kindness, I will be a messenger of God's love.

✦ When I am kind to someone in their time of need, I know God will make sure someone will be there in my time of need.

Live in the Now

CHAPTER 11

Don't Wait to Appreciate

God wants us to live in a place of gratitude, to be mindful of the beauty and incredible value He has placed on our lives. Life is not just about the destination, but also about what we do, who we know, and how we live along the way. No one wants to look back in regret because they overlooked the simple things in life or took for granted the ones they loved. To be the exceptional you that God created you to be, open your eyes to what is right in front of you and live in gratitude every single day.

Have you heard the eighties classic "Don't Know What You Got (Till It's Gone)"? Maybe it was such a popular song because it talks about a feeling that is relatable to so many of us. While the song focuses on a relationship, the lyrics can be applied to anything: our health, our family, any blessing that we are blind to until it is taken away. It's unfortunate that sometimes we have to lose something in order to recognize what it means to us.

I have a good friend who started a company on his own with a small amount of money and a lot of hope. Through hard work and long hours, he turned it into one of the largest companies of its kind in Houston. His wife is also a good friend of mine, and for several years she would complain to me about his long hours, that he was always at the office or with clients. Even when they went on family vacations, he would spend hours on the phone taking care of business. He missed the kids' ball games and music recitals and was never there to help with homework or school projects.

One day, everything changed. He was diagnosed with cancer.

The cancer had already progressed significantly, and he was told that he faced an uphill battle. All of a sudden, everything that he had taken for granted was in jeopardy. Would he still be around for his children's graduations? Would he be able to continue to provide for his wife? His business, which had taken so much of his focus, no longer seemed to be so important now that he didn't know how much longer he would live.

Thankfully, his treatments were successful, the cancer went into remission, and he recovered. However, he and his family were never the same. His challenge, like most in our lives, taught him something important. He woke up to the true value of time and how we should spend it.

Shortly after he received the good news, I saw him at church. He walked up to me and gave me a hug and told me about how much he had gained from that experience. "Let me tell you, Victoria, while those were some scary days, I now have a greater appreciation of the gifts in my life. Today I view my life completely differently than I did before I was diagnosed. I know that the most important things in my life are the people I love. When you've faced the reality of your death, you realize that a bucket list is overrated. Experiencing and appreciating what you have every day is what's truly important."

He was no longer going to take his health for granted or

prioritize his business over his family. He knew that it was those moments of family dinners, baseball games, recitals, and homework at the kitchen table that added up to a life of value. He didn't want to miss out anymore on the everyday joys that were waiting for him, that for so many years just passed him by unnoticed, unclaimed, and unappreciated.

A few weeks later, I saw his wife. She too had experienced a shift in attitude. She said, "All those years that he was building his company, I could only see the ways he wasn't around and I missed him. When I realized that cancer could take him from me for good, that he would literally never come home, I didn't care so much about the hours in the office or the phone calls during vacation. I was just glad that he was still with us."

We shouldn't have to almost lose something to appreciate how special it is. We need to guard against the tendency to become so comfortable and accustomed to the blessings in our life that we take them for granted.

What You Take for Granted, Someone Else Is Praying For

Several years ago, a family member gave me a sculpture as a housewarming gift. It was not something I would have picked out for myself, but it was distinctive and elegant and I displayed it in the corner of our living room. When Christmas arrived, I decided that I wanted to put my Christmas tree where the sculpture was standing, so I moved the sculpture into the back of a storage closet and covered it with a sheet. I fully intended to return it to its place after the holiday. Two years later, I opened that same closet and noticed the sheet. For a moment I couldn't remember what was under it. When I pulled off the sheet, I saw the sculpture. I had completely forgotten about it and had left it hiding in the back of that closet for years.

A few days later, I was working with some friends on a project at the church. We were setting up a display table, but it felt like something was missing. One of my friends said, "We need something special on this table to really make it stand out."

I immediately thought of the sculpture sitting in my closet. So I called my son, and an hour later, he arrived with the sculpture and placed it on the table. My friends exclaimed, "Oh my goodness, that is perfect. What a beautiful sculpture."

I stood back, examined it, and thought, *It really is beautiful, isn't it?*

One of my friends then said, "I know that work." She walked behind the table, examined the back of the sculpture, and exclaimed, "I thought so. This is a limited edition. I love this artist's work."

As I drove away from the church, I realized I'd never really considered the artist who made the sculpture. When I got home, I went online to see if I could find out more about him. I was shocked to see that not only was the artist quite famous, but also that my sculpture was in fact a limited edition, rare and valuable. I even found several art galleries and collectors who were seeking to buy this specific piece to add to their collections.

After the event, I brought the sculpture back home and examined it more closely. I noticed its meticulous detail and imagined the time the artist took to create it. I finally was appreciating it for how beautiful it was, and what a gift it was to have in my house. I wondered, *How did I miss the beauty that was right in front of me all along?*

As you might imagine, I don't cover it with a sheet any longer. Today I display it prominently in our home where everyone who visits can appreciate it.

What or who are you underappreciating today? Is it your job, your spouse, or a friend who's always been there for you? What you're covering with a sheet could be exactly what someone else is praying for.

Your family can't be replaced. They are one of a kind. Good friends are rare. Many people would love to have that job of yours. Don't neglect the precious things in your life. Don't get so used to them that you forget how special they truly are. The happiest people are those who appreciate the blessings in their lives and don't underestimate their value.

> *The happiest people are those who appreciate the blessings in their lives and don't underestimate their value.*

The last thing you want to do is lose something or someone just because you took them for granted, neglected them, or mistreated them. The old saying "One man's junk is another man's treasure" is true. There is always someone with less than you who would love to have the person or thing you are ignoring. Look closely at the people God's placed in your life, and rediscover the virtue, the value, and the beauty in them. Do it, before someone else does.

Count Your Kisses

Have you ever bought something like a new piece of furniture, the latest smartphone, or perhaps a new car? For the first few weeks, you were so excited about it and loved having it. But over time, you got used to it. The new thing starts to become commonplace.

We can do that with our relationships as well. We become accustomed to them, no longer in awe of how special they are. In those early days, when you fall in love with someone, you don't take them for granted. You're so excited that you've found them and you want to spend every minute of your day with them. That feeling may not last forever, but we can make a conscious effort to appreciate the many gifts right in front of us.

Joel and I aren't any different from other couples. We've been married for over thirty years, and we have stayed together because we found ways to ensure that we are appreciating each other and what we bring into one another's lives. This doesn't just happen. We work at it. If we aren't conscientious, we can get pulled in different directions and work can divert our attention away from each other.

For example, Joel and I get busy preparing for the weekend services throughout the week. We have responsibilities to our congregation and our staff. Just like you, we work and raise a family. If we aren't careful, we could look up and realize we'd hardly spent any quality time with each other for weeks on end.

So, we stay mindful of this. We take breaks from our work to see each other during the week. We may go for a bike ride or take walks together. Sometimes we will just get out and drive and enjoy each other's company.

Don't get so busy or focused on tasks that you and your spouse become strangers who just happen to live together. God doesn't want you to get accustomed to your spouse and lose the joy of what you have together. Remember that they are a gift God has given you and He wants you to cherish, honor, and love them.

When you stay focused on what a gift that person is to you, you realize that you are called to enjoy that gift. I'm not just saying spend time together; I'm saying spend quality time together. Quality time doesn't have to be an expensive vacation or a lavish dinner out. Quality time means gentle, loving, and respectful time spent in each other's presence.

Too often the time we spend with our spouse is focused on tasks and to-do lists, checking our emails and talking about what needs to get done. Quality time is not just about talking. It is about appreciating, and loving, and recognizing the beautiful gifts that person brings into your life.

I read an article recently where several thousand people were asked to name the single most important quality in a marriage. Some of the people had successful marriages and some did not. Pretty much all of the people who had gotten divorced said they wished they had focused more on communication. Typical responses were "We quit communicating," or "They didn't listen to me," or "It was like we were talking past each other."

Communicating is important and every marriage counselor will tell you how essential it is. But communication is not all that is needed. The respondents who had been in marriages lasting twenty, thirty, and even forty years also focused on one characteristic. They focused on respect. They shared comments like "We miscommunicate all the time, but we never treat each other with disrespect," or "There's a lot we don't agree on, but we always respectfully agree to disagree." They acknowledged that communication will always break down at one point or another, but if you can maintain your level of respect in the relationship, you'll always be able to move past the miscommunication.

When you respect someone or something, you recognize its

value. If someone gave you a precious heirloom or something of great value, you would take care of it. You wouldn't put it in a drawer where you throw your keys and miscellaneous items. You wouldn't store it in a closet with the vacuum cleaner and brooms. You would have a special place where it couldn't be harmed or broken. You would go to great lengths to make sure it was taken care of. I've learned what you value you respect. When you value your spouse, your children, you don't throw words around that you don't mean. You're not careless with how you treat them. You respect them because you know how valuable they are. You realize they're not ordinary; they're not common. They are precious, gifts from God.

To respect something means to esteem, look up to, revere, and honor. To respect your spouse means you know they are a blessing in your life and you do not take them for granted. You prioritize the relationship and honor your spouse for what they bring to your life.

No one intends to disrespect their spouse, but it can happen over time through arguments, frustrations, and small moments of criticism. If your spouse has ever told you that you're too critical of them, they're probably right. The next time you notice one of their faults, catch yourself before you start complaining. Nobody likes to see their faults put on display. First off, they're not blind to their own blemishes even if you think they are. When you point them out, it just makes them feel like a failure in their own eyes, and the last thing you want is a partner who doesn't respect him- or herself. Any psychologist can tell you that the more someone loves themselves, the better able they are to love others. Those small moments of what you deem to be correction can feel critical and cause the respect in your relationship to erode.

Another way that disrespect can surface is in the heat of an argument. The old saying "All is fair in love and war" does not apply to arguments with your spouse. You are not at war with your spouse nor should you ever be, even if it sometimes feels like it. You are on the same team. God joined you together.

If you've fallen into this trap already, put the brakes on it. Make a decision that you will never disrespect your spouse again. You shouldn't allow anyone to disrespect your spouse, including you.

Keep respect alive and well in your relationship by staying focused on what a gift that person is to you. Don't wait until something is gone to appreciate it and honor it.

> *Don't wait until something is gone to appreciate it and honor it.*

When I was growing up, our family knew this very sweet couple. The woman was always encouraging people. Every time I saw her, she wore a smile on her face. Last year, after a long marriage and living well into her eighties, she passed away. I attended her funeral and went up to console her husband. Despite the sad day, he had joy in his heart. He told me about how he'd had a heart attack fifteen years prior. While he was in the hospital, his wife said, "Honey, this just shows us how fragile life really is. I could have lost you. From now on, I want to start doing something special. Every night before we go to bed, I want us to kiss seven times just to show how much we love each other. Just so we don't take each other for granted."

He told me that his wife picked the number seven because it represented their perfect love for each other. So, for more than fifteen years, they never went to sleep without kissing each other seven times.

In a day when marriages are often discarded on a whim, he had his memory of a thousand kisses to assure him that he had found his true love and he had valued her every day. It made his memory of her perfect.

That woman went to be with the Lord on a Tuesday, but Monday night she had kissed her husband seven times. She had no regrets, and she left him with none. She wasn't too busy and she was never too upset. She realized that there was no such thing as an ordinary day. That's the way I want to live.

You never know when you or someone you love is going to be gone. This is not an ordinary day. Let the people in your life know that they are special and that you appreciate them. Tell them how much you love them. Spend quality time together because today is a special day. It's unique. It's irreplaceable. Its hours may be used or misused, invested or wasted. Appreciate today and all that it can bring to your life.

Choose to See the Good

When we face difficulties, it can be hard to stay grateful or difficult to appreciate each day. But what a shame to come to the end of your life and realize, "I spent most of my life worried and upset." God wants us to develop new mind-sets that will help us stay grateful through good times and bad. Things may not be going perfectly in your life, but the fact is, this is the day the Lord has made. You are not here by accident. There's nothing going on in your life that God is not aware of. There is no situation that's too difficult for Him to turn around, but you have to do your part and give Him something to work with. God works where there's an attitude of faith. Be grateful and stay at peace. No matter what comes against you, find the good.

> *God works where there's an attitude of faith.*

I heard a story about Bill Bright, the founder of Campus Crusade for Christ, which is today called Cru. Toward the end of his life, he developed an incurable lung disease. It was very painful and there was no treatment. The cancer was literally eating away the lining of his lungs. Finally, it got to the point where he couldn't leave his house. He was bedridden. Here was a man who spent over sixty years of his adult life traveling the world doing so much good, and now he couldn't get out of bed. It seemed unfair for his life to end in such a disheartening way.

A few weeks before he died, one of his friends went to see him.

He sat by Dr. Bright's bed and said, "Dr. Bright, I'm so sorry to see you suffering. I'm so sorry to see you in this condition."

In a frail and broken voice, Bill Bright responded, "No, I'm not suffering. I'm in an air-conditioned room. I'm in a soft bed. I have the best care in the world."

Many people in that situation would have been down and discouraged, but Dr. Bright chose to be grateful. He chose to find the positive. His attitude was *As long as I'm able to breathe, I'm going to find something for which to be thankful.* When I hear a story like that, it makes me appreciate what I have.

> *No matter what difficulty we may be facing or what is coming against us, we need to be grateful people and train ourselves to appreciate every day and find the good.*

No matter what difficulty we may be facing or what is coming against us, we need to be grateful people and train ourselves to appreciate every day and find the good.

I heard a story about two men who were sharing a room in the hospital. Both men were confined to their beds, unable to get up and move about. The man closest to the window developed the habit of telling the other man what he saw outside.

He would explain in great detail, "Today, I see a beautiful sunrise, the kids are out playing, and the trees are blooming." Every day the other man would listen with great interest. It was the highlight of his day.

This went on for several weeks until the gentleman by the window became very ill and was moved to another wing of the hospital. His friend was greatly saddened that he wasn't there anymore and he missed knowing what was going on outside. One afternoon he asked the nurse if he could have the bed by the window. He couldn't wait to see all those life-giving scenes, scenes that reminded him of the beauty of the world, and how much was going on outside the hospital walls.

As the nurse carefully moved him to his new bed, he settled in and then turned his gaze to the window. But all he could see was a brick wall.

He called the nurse back in and said, "What's going on? For weeks, my friend described what he saw out the window. He talked about the sunset and seeing kids playing and the beautiful pattern of the clouds. I can't see anything but this brick wall."

The nurse smiled and said, "Didn't you know your friend was blind? He was seeing it all with his heart."

God has given us this life so we can enjoy it. We can choose to see the good, the bad, or nothing at all. We will all face hardships. We will shoulder many responsibilities, but that doesn't mean we can't take the time to see the value in every day and in every gift God has given.

Don't become blind to the blessings God has given you. When you see through the eyes of a grateful heart, you will appreciate all the beauty that lies around you. Life is fragile. Find reasons to be grateful. They are always there if you look for them.

EXCEPTIONAL THOUGHTS

✦ I will look around and thank God for the blessings in my life each and every day. I will live in a place of gratitude and be mindful of the beauty and incredible value He has placed in my life. I will enjoy my journey—valuing the people in my life and living with enthusiasm along the way.

✦ I will guard against the tendency to become so accustomed to the blessings in my life that I take them for granted. I will remember that what's truly important is experiencing and appreciating what I have every day.

✦ My family is irreplaceable, good friends are rare, and many people would love to have my life. I will not neglect these precious gifts or forget how special and valuable they are to me.

✦ I will remember to respect those I love, to honor them, and to take care of them. I will spend quality time building and maintaining a strong, healthy relationship.

✦ I will remember that when disagreements arise, to disagree respectfully. I will keep the lines of communication open and the integrity of the relationship a priority.

✦ I will look for ways to bring an attitude of gratitude into all aspects of my life. And to practice being grateful in the good times and bad. I will find my own way to count the kisses and to remember to soak up and truly appreciate every day.

CHAPTER 12

─────────

Make Every Season Count

When my daughter was a senior in high school, she, like many of her peers, spent countless hours carefully preparing college applications. She perfected her resume, wrote application letters, devoted hours to her essays. Finally, it was time to submit them and pray that all those hours of preparation would lead to an acceptance letter. Administrators and teachers told the students that it would take two to three months before they would receive any response.

When you are seventeen years old, what college you go to is the biggest decision of your life. The anticipation was agonizing for these young people. Those two months seemed to drag on, and then it was three months. As time went by, the questions lingering in their minds seemed to intensify. They evolved from *What school will I attend?* to *What if I don't get accepted to the one I really want to go to? Who will I live with if you get accepted and I don't?* On and on, the questions swirled in their heads. It seemed the longer they waited, the more questions crept in and the more doubt began to form. The wait was causing them to get weary and frustrated. They would check their computers daily to see if their acceptance letter had been posted. They were so consumed with the outcome, trying to figure it all out, anticipate what was to come, that their once carefree days became filled with stress and worry, keeping them from truly enjoying what was taking place in their lives at the time.

It's like the process of a caterpillar becoming a lovely butterfly. As it is trying to emerge out of its cocoon there is a waiting period. It takes time and effort. But once that butterfly finally makes its way out, it's beautiful, it's strong, and it's ready to take flight. God wants us to understand that whatever season we are facing right now, we're getting stronger and more beautiful, and He's preparing us to take flight to the next stage of our lives.

After three long months of checking her computer every day to see the results of her application, my daughter finally got the answer she was hoping for and was able to attend the university she really wanted. She was so thrilled, but the waiting wasn't over. As she looked forward to attending in the fall, she had to wait to see what sorority she would be invited to join. Then she waited to see who her roommates would be, and she waited to see what her classes would be like. She will be waiting to graduate, waiting to get a job, waiting to see whom she marries, waiting to have children. Wait, wait, and wait. She is a young girl, so she has a lot of waiting to do. Waiting is one of the most challenging aspects of our lives. It is no fun to wait.

If you are waiting for something, keep the right perspective. Don't look at it like you can't be happy until it happens. You can be happy now, knowing you're developing your wings. You are growing, maturing, and getting ready to take flight. Even if things don't turn out the way you would like them to, God knows what He is doing. He is going to get you to the right place.

A few of my daughter's friends didn't receive letters of acceptance from their first-choice schools. They were accepted to their second choices. But today, after having been enrolled for three years, they all would tell you that they are *exactly* where they are supposed to be. They are glad they didn't get into the school they thought they wanted. They are growing, thriving, and preparing for the new seasons ahead right where they are. It is amazing how God knows what is best for us.

> It is *amazing how God knows what is best for us.*

Today, looking back, each of those girls would say, "I don't know why I was so anxious and worried. If I would have known then what I know now, I would have relaxed instead of being so preoccupied about the future."

Wait Well for Your "Not Yet Happenings"

Life is a process of waiting. That's why it is important for us to learn to wait the right way. As we go through the different seasons, it seems like we're always in a hurry to get to our next destination. And while we all have goals, things we want to accomplish, situations we'd like to see change, without realizing it we can put off our own happiness by becoming consumed with where we'd like to be. We get preoccupied with the "not yet happenings" of our lives. We become so focused on things to come that we don't enjoy the season we're in right now.

Patience is defined as "the capacity to accept or tolerate delay, trouble, or suffering without getting angry or upset." It is something we strive to teach our children; be patient, we say, as they wait for dinner, as they wait in line, as they wait for Christmas. Patience is about waiting well. Being willing to let things come in their own time without grumbling and frustration and doubt. I have prayed for young women who want to be married so badly that they are missing out on what God is doing in their lives right now. They are so consumed with who they are going to marry that they don't enjoy the season that they are in right now.

If that's you today, I want to encourage you to relax. Trust God's timing. Yes, pray for God's hand to be guiding you, be excited about the future, but remember that in the waiting there is a preparation that is taking place. You are growing and becoming for the next season of life. God didn't intend for us to give up during the dry seasons, during the seasons when we are waiting for our prayers to be answered. He wants us to develop and persevere in those times. While you're waiting to find the right person, make sure you're becoming the right person. Develop the traits of the person you would want to marry. When we learn to wait well, we will strengthen our muscle of patience and that's when we will see the promise come to pass.

> *God didn't intend for us to give up during the dry seasons, during the seasons when we are waiting for our prayers to be answered.*

Hebrews 6 says through faith and patience we will inherit the promises (see v. 12). I don't know about you, but it seems that we start out great when our dreams and desires are fresh in our heart, when the seed is just planted. We have faith to believe it will happen. But it is during those days when we stare at the earth and still see no signs of life that we lose our way. When things take longer than we expect and we don't see anything happening, we lose our patience. We start to complain and get frustrated. God isn't making us wait to harm us. He is developing the power of patience. Patience means you know that you can trust God no matter how long it takes. It's the key ingredient to waiting well. Oftentimes we think we can't be happy until what we are waiting on comes to

> *Patience means you know that you can trust God no matter how long it takes.*

pass. That is putting a timeline on your happiness. God wants us to be content right where we are. When we are content knowing that God is in control and we stay in peace, all the pieces of our life will fall into place.

Your Harvest Is Coming

No one is exempt from the waiting process. When we hear that word *wait*, we think about folding our hands and doing nothing. It feels boring and passive. The Amplified Bible gives us a clearer understanding of the "wait" in Scripture. It says: Those who expect, who hope, who look for God's goodness (see Isa. 40:31 AMP). That is how you wait in faith, actively looking for God's goodness everyday. Expecting His blessing and favor. Believing for a turnaround in your family, your health, and your job. There is anticipation in your heart.

The writer of James gives us this example of waiting well. "See how the farmer waits for the land to yield its valuable crop, patiently waiting for the autumn and spring rains. You too, be patient and stand firm" (James 5:7–8). The farmer doesn't doubt the crops are going to come up. He isn't digging up his seed, making sure it is still there. He is looking for the rains, he is looking for signs of the season changing, anticipating and getting ready for the harvest. He doesn't let the fact that he can't *see* any changes cause him to lose his joy and enthusiasm. The wait builds his strength, patience, and character, because he knows it's just a matter of time before the harvest. Waiting with expectancy is waiting actively. You are praying, believing, and preparing for it to happen.

Like the farmer, you've planted. You've prayed. You've watered your seed. You've thanked God. You can have the confidence that says, "Not *if* it happens but *when* it happens." In the same way that you know the sun is going to come up in the morning, you have to know that what God promised you is going to come to pass. It may happen today. It may happen next week or next year. But like that farmer, you too can anticipate with joy that your harvest is on its way.

> *In the same way that you know the sun is going to come up in the morning, you have to know that what God promised you is going to come to pass.*

I was in an elevator with my daughter one day, and when we stopped at a floor and the doors opened, a man walked in and then looked at me in surprise. I said hello. While he continued to look at me, he said, "I can't believe you are standing in this elevator. I was praying this morning that God would strengthen me and help me develop patience. I have something I am waiting to happen in my business, and I feel like God is asking me to wait until it is His timing. I love your ministry and I am so encouraged by it that I am taking this as a sign that God is still at work and I need to continue to stand firm and be patient." I thanked the man for sharing that with me and thanked God for using me to encourage him during the wait. That man was wise like the farmer. He was waiting with expectancy. Looking for a sign. Believing that what God promised him was on the way.

Prepared in the Waiting

God is always at work in our lives. Even during the wait, He is active. He is nurturing and strengthening and preparing and encouraging. Even when we don't see it, and others may question what we are doing with our lives. A friend of mine told me about a time when she was eighteen years old, and she had offered to deliver dinner to a guest minister's family. Upon entering the small apartment they were staying in while in town, she saw a mom with two small boys, one on each hip, while two older boys were running up and down the stairs in the midst of a loud, energetic game. The mother smiled at my friend and asked that she place the dinner on the table in the kitchen. She then thanked her for her kindness, and turned to get her children cleaned up for dinner.

As my friend walked out the door, she thought to herself: *That poor mother. Four kids and running ragged, racing around just trying to keep up with errands and demands of motherhood.*

Not me, she said to herself, *I have too many dreams and goals to achieve for my life. That mother will never be able to dream again. Not with all the responsibilities of running a house.*

Years passed, and after dozing off momentarily in her bath, exhausted from trying to keep up with her three young children, my friend began to wonder if she had missed out on the dreams that she once had. As she began to contemplate her life and the season she was in, her thoughts went back to that day she was eighteen years old and delivering a meal to a young mother whose life she never wanted to have. Now my friend realized she had become "that" mother. But now she understood more fully who that mother was and what was happening in her life at that time. Despite her thoughts and opinions that day, that frazzled mother had gone on to become an international in-demand speaker and bestselling author. That "poor mother" was Lisa Bevere.

My friend was encouraged that there would come a time when her desires and dreams could rise to the surface again. That she too was in the midst of a sometimes-exhausting season of raising up champion children. But that season wouldn't last forever. Lisa Bevere had raised those kids while building her character, resolve, and strength, and then she entered the next season of her life. The selfless sacrifice of mothering did not disqualify her from her dreams; they prepared her for her dreams. Those years were necessary for the amazing harvest to come. Not only does she have a beautiful family, but they are all doing ministry together.

> We will renew our strength when we are actively *waiting on God.*

If we look back at the example in James, and we think about what a farmer is doing while he is waiting for the harvest, he doesn't sit around passively for months and months. While he's waiting, he sharpens his tools. He makes sure his tractor and equipment are maintained and ready to go. He calls his suppliers and gets everything lined up. He hasn't seen one plant come up out of the ground. The whole field looks completely empty, yet he's making all kinds of preparations for the harvest that he knows is coming. He has such confidence that he's putting actions behind his faith. That's what it means to wait like a farmer. You're not just hoping. You're not just praying. You're getting prepared, taking steps of faith. Scripture says to wait upon the Lord, and He will renew your strength (see Isa. 40:31). We will renew our strength when we are *actively* waiting on God. Preparing ourselves in the wait. Knowing that this season is preparing us for the next.

Be Patient and Trust God's Timing

God wants us to have goals, He wants us to dream big, but we have to trust His timing.

> *God wants us to have goals, He wants us to dream big, but we have to trust His timing.*

I talked to a man who runs a multi-million-dollar company. He told me how faithful God had been. And then he pulled a small piece of paper out of his wallet. He said, "God has been good to me even when times were tough. I've always tried to remember that He was at work in my life, and hold on to the truth that while I was waiting for something to happen, He was preparing me for something great. The seed had been planted, I needed to be patient to develop my roots." He then showed me the piece of paper, and on it was a list of jobs. This man had written down all the jobs he had worked since he was young. When he was thirteen, he was a paperboy. At fifteen, he started mowing lawns, and he added snow removal when he was seventeen. In college, he was a plumber's helper, then a pipefitter's helper, and then a contractor. The list went on and on.

I thought, *My goodness, how many jobs has he had?*

The man said he created the list for a special purpose. When he was facing yet another job change, he wanted to encourage himself. "I went back through my life and thought about every job I ever had. And I asked myself: 'What did that job teach me? What skills did that job give me? What roots did it develop in me so that I could be stronger and more firm for the next assignment?'"

He realized he had learned something valuable at every job that had prepared him for where God was taking him. He even went so far as to assign a word to each of those jobs, such as "commitment," "perseverance," "integrity," and "responsibility."

He said, "Victoria, at the time, some of those jobs didn't make any sense. They were difficult, dirty, and exhausting. I felt I was ready to move on to something bigger. But the list reminds me how God was directing my steps and how each job was necessary."

Sometimes we have a tendency during the wait to stop waiting on God and start making things happen for ourselves. I think about the Israelites when Moses had led them out of Egypt and they were on their way to the Promised Land. Moses left them at the camp when he went up to meet with God on Mount Sinai. He told them he would be back. But the Israelites grew impatient when Moses didn't come back with an answer from God as quickly as they expected. They began to doubt Moses would return and decided that they would take the gold that God had given them and make idols they could worship. They took control of the situation instead of trusting that God was going to move at the right time.

We can all have a tendency to be like the Israelites, to feel like we need to take things into our own hands. But God has a way and a time. Can you trust that He will bring it about?

Live Each Day in Joyful Expectation

In our society, we have lost the power that patience has to offer. In this digital age, we can do things at the click of a mouse or the tap of a button. Shopping online, sending a message to another country in a matter of seconds, checking the weather anywhere in the world. We are accustomed to getting answers to questions immediately. God doesn't work that way. We have to be careful so that we don't get so caught up in instant gratification that we become impatient.

Jesus told five hundred disciples: "Wait here in Jerusalem because the Holy Spirit is going to come upon you." He added, "Don't leave. Wait for it to happen." Do you know that only 120 out of the five hundred disciples didn't get impatient and leave? Three hundred and fifty men left because they didn't have the patience to wait. Sometimes when something takes a long time to come to fruition, we get bored. We lose our enthusiasm. We forget what we're waiting for. We quit expecting. We can miss out on so much when we cannot be patient. The disciples who stayed that day got renewed, recharged, and energized by the Holy Spirit. They received what they were waiting for and had been promised.

God wants the wait not to weaken us but to strengthen us. He wants to surprise us with His goodness. Just like winter gives way to spring, the wait will give way to the good things

> *God wants the wait not to weaken us but to strengthen us.*

of God. God is going to release what you are waiting for at just the right time. And when He does you are going to be stronger and more determined to stay the course.

I believe that in the days ahead, you will be reminiscing about the days you're in now. You will look back on the waiting and be able to see how it was preparing you, how it was strengthening you, how it was giving you roots and nourishment to be strong for what was to come. Relax and say with the Psalmist, "God, my times are in Your hands" (see Ps. 31:15). Believe with confidence that God is at work. Live each day in joyful expectation. And know that one day, the wait will be over.

Every time I go to the doctor's office, I sit in the waiting room with the other patients. Even if the wait goes on longer than I want it to, I stay in my chair because I know it is only a matter of time before it is my turn. I expect that eventually the nurse will call my name, because she has every time. If you are in the waiting room of life, hoping for things to change, waiting for your prayers to be answered, stay in the chair. Don't give up. Persevere and stand firm in your faith. You are going to see it happen in God's perfect timing. If you will develop in the time you are waiting, if you will wait with expectancy and joy, and not give in to complaining or allow doubt to enter your mind, this time will not be wasted. God is preparing you. Stay the course. When you are in God's waiting room, it is only a matter of time before He will call your name.

❦

EXCEPTIONAL THOUGHTS

✦ God is at work in my life today. He knows where I am and the process I'm going through. I will not get so focused on the "not yet happenings" of my life that I don't enjoy the season I'm in right now.

✦ I am growing, maturing, and being prepared to take flight to the next stage of my life. God has placed in me everything I need to fulfill my destiny, so I am looking for signs of His goodness and favor, anticipating the harvest to come.

✦ I will actively wait upon the Lord and walk in His strength knowing that this season is preparing me. I believe God is going to release what I am waiting for at just the right time, and I will be ready.

✦ Every day I will say with the Psalmist, "God, my times are in Your hands." I will believe that God is at work, and I will live each day in joyful expectation and with a grateful heart, knowing that God is faithful.

SECTION VII

Power Up

CHAPTER 13

Draw Close to God

Several years ago, I went to a play with some friends at the Wortham Theater here in Houston. Our seats were near the back, making it difficult to see or hear the actors. Unfortunately, we had only one pair of binoculars to share between the five of us, so we took turns using them. When I didn't have them, I felt totally disconnected from the action and found it difficult to follow the story. When my turn would come to use the binoculars, I would draw them up to my eyes, focus in, and suddenly I would feel like I was a part of the story. I could see the expressions on the actors' faces, and I could hear them better because I knew which actor was speaking. With the binoculars, I felt like I was onstage with them. What was once far away had been drawn close.

The apostle Paul says, "But now in Christ Jesus you who once were far away have been brought near by the blood of Christ" (Eph. 2:13). You may have felt far away from God at times during your life, but He always has you in His sight. God has His binoculars focused on you. He is in your story. We just have to realize that He is as close as the very breath that we breathe. Any distance between us and God has been closed through Jesus.

Experts say there are an estimated 7.6 billion people living on our planet. When we consider this, it is easy to feel isolated and insignificant. It can feel as though we're just one inconsequential person among billions. But don't give in to those feelings. If we do, we will find ourselves feeling so far away from God that we'll believe He doesn't know us or care about where we are or what is going on in our lives. If this is how you are feeling, I want you to know that God is up close and personal with you today.

To live your exceptional life, come close to Him so you can be reminded who you really are, His beloved child. Just like at the end of a school day, when your kids may climb into your lap to tell you about the good and bad that happened while you were separated, God is your loving Father and wants you to crawl into His lap. He knows all that you've been through but He still wants you to draw near.

Many people think they need to change their lives before they come to God. But we can't clean up our own lives. We can't bring the change that God wants to bring in our lives. God had to come to us through Jesus. As the apostle Paul said, "While we were still sinners, Christ died for us" (Rom. 5:8). Only Jesus Christ can change your life. There's no mess that you've made that He can't help you clean up. There is nothing that God cannot do for you. There's nothing on the inside of you that would make you distant from God. In Jesus, you are made right with God. He loves you just the way you are, and He came to you just the way you are.

Whatever you're facing today, don't let anything stand between you and God. No matter what you feel or what you've done, He wants a relationship with you. God wants you to know: "I'm right here with you. I'm an up-close-and-personal God and I want to be in your story."

Up Close and Personal

The Bible tells many stories of just how up close and personal God wants to be. Jesus and His disciples were traveling from Judea to Galilee, when Jesus made an unexpected announcement. He said, "I have to go through Samaria." This statement surprised His disciples because, although Samaria was on the way to Galilee, at that time the Jewish people took the long way around Samaria in order to avoid the Samaritans. The disciples didn't understand why Jesus would break with tradition. Unknown to the disciples, Jesus had a divine appointment with a Samaritan woman.

Around noon, this Samaritan woman walked up to the village well with her watering jar. Most of the other women in the village came to the well in the morning when it was cooler, but this woman waited until noon—the hottest part of the day—in order to avoid the others. In the story we discover that she was a woman who had a bad reputation. So she chose to come to the well alone to avoid the rejection and ridicule of the others.

When she arrived this day, she found Jesus waiting for her. He asked her for a drink of water. She could tell that Jesus was a Jew and was surprised that He would not only associate with her, a Samaritan, but also that He would drink water that she drew from the well.

This woman wanted to stay isolated in her shame, but Jesus had come to draw her near. As He continued to speak to her, she carefully eased a little closer and began to listen to what He was saying. After inquiring about her life, He revealed to her that He already knew everything about her. He knew that she had been married five times and that she was currently living with a man who was not her husband.

That day, Jesus drew close to a woman filled with shame who was living out a multitude of bad choices, and He offered her salvation. She came to draw water to quench her thirst that day. Jesus offered her "living water" that would quench her thirst forever. She felt the incredible closeness of a personal God Who was saying, "I know everything about you—every sin, every mistake, every bad choice—yet, I still love you."

This is what I love about Jesus. Just like He told His disciples, "I need to go through Samaria," He "needed" to come to us and give His life for us. He broke protocol to get to the Samaritan woman, and He broke through every barrier to get to us.

God hasn't brought us close because we're doing things right. He comes to us to offer us salvation. The beautiful part is that we can receive Him just as we are. Our faults, mistakes, and wrongdoings don't drive Him away; they draw Him closer. He's offering the living water of eternal life, and all we have to do is say yes and receive it freely.

> *Our faults, mistakes, and wrongdoings don't drive Him away; they draw Him closer.*

There is another interesting part to the story. Jesus chose this woman to be the first person to whom He would reveal His identity as the Messiah. He had yet to tell anyone, not even His close disciples, that He was the Son of God. Yet, this woman at the well, who had brought upon herself shame and dishonor, was found worthy in the eyes of Jesus to be the first to know Him in a way that no one else did.

Unlike others who later in Jesus' life would disbelieve Him, this Samaritan woman understood that she was in the presence of God. She didn't have to see Him turn the water to wine to believe. She just knew and she wanted everything He had for her.

She was so moved by this revelation that she ran back into town to tell everyone about this man. "Come meet a man at the well who knows everything I've ever done and yet He loves me."

This woman had been an outcast. People had shunned and ridiculed her. But she was so moved by her encounter with Jesus that she forgot her shame and ran to tell the good news to the very people who scorned her. This brokenhearted woman, who had been crushed by the trials of life, did not care what they thought. She only wanted them to experience the same love that she felt. That's what happens when you have a close encounter with God. You throw away the shame and the failures and you want to share your newfound freedom with everyone. The Bible says that because of her testimony, "Many of the Samaritans from that town believed in Him."

The Psalmist says, "The LORD is close to the brokenhearted and saves those who are crushed in spirit" (Ps. 34:18). He doesn't shun you, criticize you, or look at what you're doing wrong. He won't throw His hands up and walk away just because you make a mistake. Instead, He draws near to you in love. Even in your worst times, He will offer you His living water. He is drawing near to you even now. Let go of the shame and every negative label that people have put on you, and believe that He is the One Who desires to draw near to you, to heal your broken heart, and to fill your thirsty soul.

God Is Watching You

I have a good friend who is a pastor here in town, who told me an interesting story. He said that he went out to get the newspaper one morning and he saw a baby owl lying in the grass. He called to his young children and they ran outside to see it. They wanted to pick the baby owl up and hold it, but he cautioned them not to until he found out more about it. He called the local veterinarian and told her about the baby owl and asked her what to do. The vet said that strong winds can sometimes blow a baby owl out of its nest. Other times the baby will get overconfident and try to fly before it's able.

"In any case," she said, "you don't want to touch the owl or try to pick it up."

"Why?" my friend asked.

The vet said, "If you look up in the trees, there's a good chance you will see the mama owl watching her baby owl."

With the veterinarian still on the phone, the pastor and his children went back outside and looked around. Just as she had predicted, they saw this huge mama owl at the top of a pine tree, her big eyes staring right back at them. It was like she was on guard, standing at attention just ready to swoop down and defend her baby.

When he told the vet that they could see the mama owl, she said, "If you touch that baby owl, that mama owl will do everything she can to protect it, even if it means giving her own life."

The good news is your Heavenly Father is watching over you right now. The strong winds may have blown you out of the nest, you may have gotten knocked down, you may feel alone, but if you'll just look up, you'll see His heavenly eyes staring right back at you, waiting to defend you, to protect you, to show you His favor.

You're a Child of the Promise

Whenever I read the stories of Jesus' interactions with different people, I am always amazed by how He treated everyone as significant and valued, how He seemed to see people with different eyes, worthy of His undivided love and attention.

Jesus was teaching in a synagogue on the Sabbath. There was a large crowd gathered around Him, listening intently to His words. Suddenly, He stopped speaking and took notice of one solitary woman among them. She wasn't beautiful or flamboyant or dazzling in any way. The Bible says she "had been crippled by a spirit for eighteen years." In fact, she was bent completely forward and could not straighten up. However, Jesus noticed her.

When she came into the synagogue that day, she might have felt completely unnoticed and alone. Certainly, most people avoided her. But Jesus saw her. In fact, He immediately stopped everything He was doing and called her to come to Him.

As that woman slowly hobbled closer to Jesus, He spoke to her, "Woman, you are set free from your infirmity today. You're free."

Then He touched her, and she immediately stood up straight for the first time in nearly two decades. All those years she'd been looking at the ground. Her world was filled with the images of dirt, rocks, and people's feet. She could probably go an entire day without seeing another person's face. But at that moment, she straightened up and she saw the face of God.

For eighteen years she had felt invisible, like no one saw her. She had felt uncared for. She had felt judged. To others she was the crippled woman, but Jesus saw who she truly was and drew her near. He saw her and called her "a daughter of Abraham." When He called her that, He was calling her a precious Daughter of the Promise who needed and deserved His compassion and love.

When He set her free that day, she was stunned. I wonder how long it took before she truly realized that she would never be crippled again. Did she wake up the next morning expecting to be bent over, only to find that she was not only set free, but also set free for good? When you've lived a certain way for so long, it's hard to believe you can be any other way. Perhaps you've been bent down under a negative attitude for a long time. You don't even realize that you too are a Child of the Promise and that God has already spoken the Word and set you free. He's already freed you from whatever would bind you, but you just don't realize it yet.

The enemy wants to keep you looking down. He doesn't want you to see ahead to a future filled with promise and hope, and he certainly doesn't want you to see the face of your Savior. He doesn't want you to see that you are a precious Child of the Promise.

But God is looking at you. He sees you, loves you, and wants to draw you near.

But God is looking at you. He sees you, loves you, and wants to draw you near.

One Sunday during a church service, I was praying for a beautiful young woman. She looked me straight in the eyes and said, "I feel so unnoticed by God. I feel as though God doesn't even care about what's going on in my life."

I believe that sometimes we all can feel that way. We've struggled with some issue for so long that we wonder, *God, where are You? Do You see what I'm going through? I've tried so hard. Do You even care?*

Sometimes we can sit in a packed auditorium and feel so alone, just a body in the crowd, wondering, *God, do You know I'm here? Do I matter?*

I'm sure that the woman who was bent over in the synagogue wondered that thousands of times over the years.

I want to tell you that right now, God's eyes are on you.

The Bible says: He knew you before the foundation of the world. He chose you in His great love for you. He says you are His precious treasure. He even counts every single hair on your head. Now that amazes me, but God is God. He said it, and I believe it, no matter how I may be feeling.

If we're going to overcome those crushing feelings of aloneness or being uncared for, we have to stir up our faith. Even if I feel alone in a crowded room, I'm going to stand on His Word: He knew me before creation. He knows my sitting down and my rising up. He knows my thoughts from afar. He knows all of my ways. There's nowhere I can go where He is not with me.

I admire the fact that the bent-over woman showed up at the synagogue that day. She didn't let her condition keep her from getting in the presence of Jesus. Too often we allow the conditions in our life to keep us from our position of faith. We can think *I'm not good enough. I'm too damaged, and I can't change. It's been too long.*

No one would have blamed that woman for staying home on that Sabbath day. But she didn't allow her condition to change her position. She was a Daughter of the Promise, and that's what kept her going.

Don't allow anything to bend you over and bind you up. God is calling you forward today. He is saying, "Whom the Son sets free is free indeed."

You Are Unforgettable

Are you feeling forgotten? Do you think that no one is watching and no one cares? God is the mama owl in the tree, watching over you with fierce love. He has not forgotten you. The phrase "God remembers you" is used seventy-three times in Scripture. This doesn't just mean that He doesn't forget you. It's more significant than that. It means He's going to surprise you with His goodness and overwhelm you with His favor. He's going to turn negative things around. When God remembers you, it means He's going to show up and show out like you've never seen before. When God turns things around, His blessings will take you to a whole new level.

Think about the story of Rachel in the Bible. She longed to have a baby but continued to be barren. Back in those days, a woman was valued for her ability to provide her husband a child, especially a son to be the heir. Her inability to conceive not only brought shame to her, but also shame to her husband, Jacob. Year after year went by and still her arms were empty. Jacob loved Rachel but she struggled with not having a child, feeling like she wasn't fulfilling her obligation to her husband. To make matters even more difficult, her sister, Leah, kept having one son after another. It was a constant reminder of her disappointment. It made her feel forgotten, so alone and empty.

One day everything changed for Rachel. Scripture says, "God

remembered Rachel" (Gen. 30:22).
Sometimes God's mercy shows up
when we don't feel like we have any
more strength to believe.

> *Sometimes God's mercy shows up when we don't feel like we have any more strength to believe.*

I am sure she felt like she
had prayed and prayed until she
couldn't pray anymore. But notice what happened: Darkness
gives way to the light.

God remembered her and gave her a child. When God remembers you, what has looked impossible is going to change. Those secret frustrations are going to give way to a blessing.

You may feel like Rachel; your dreams have been so long in coming to pass that you feel forgotten, alone, and think they are never going to happen. Maybe you've given up on finding the right person. Or your career hasn't taken off the way you thought it would; compared to others, you feel left behind. Don't give up, keep believing, keep praying. You may be ready to give up on a dream but God isn't. He still has a way to bring it to pass.

Never lose sight of the fact that the Creator of the universe is closely watching you.

God says, "I will not forget you. I have carved your name in the palms of My hands" (see Isa. 49:15–16).

The good news today is that you are not forgotten. You may have had a sickness for years. You may have been told that it's never going to change, but God hasn't forgotten about you. He sees every lonely night, and the darkness is about to give way to light.

Maybe you've had a dream of going back to college and getting your master's degree, but it doesn't seem to be coming to pass regardless of how much you try. God hasn't forgotten about you.

He still has a plan, and He's working right now to line up the right pieces that will all fit together. At the perfect time, you're going to see God do something amazing.

Maybe you have a parent who has needed your care for a long time. You're investing a lot of your extra time and energy so that they can remain in their own home. Know this: God hasn't forgotten about the dreams that you may have put on hold. He hasn't forgotten about the goals that you have. God sees everything that you're giving up, and He's telling you that He's not only going to bring you blessings but He is also going to increase you in every way.

People may treat you with shame like they did with Rachel. People may forget you or push you aside, but you're never alone. God never forgets you. You may have had people do you wrong and write you off. Someone may have left you at a time when you needed them the most, but remember the Bible says that Jesus is the friend that sticks closer than a brother (see Prov. 18:24).

When you have some bad breaks, when you pray but heaven seems silent, when the chronic pain seems to go on forever, you need to take your stand of faith and say to yourself, "God has not forgotten about me. My name is written on the palms of His hands. He has not forgotten and cannot forget about my dreams and goals. He has not forgotten about the injustices. He's promised He'll pay me back double. He'll get me to where I need to go. All those seeds I've sown, I know it's just a matter of time before I reap my harvest."

Do you remember the famous song by Nat King Cole called "Unforgettable"? That's what I'm saying today—you are unforgettable to God. You are the apple of His eye. All through the day He's looking at you. When He sees you, He says, "That's My child. That's My masterpiece. I'm proud of that man. That young person brings a smile to my face. That single parent brings joy to My heart. I see that person is discouraged, but I haven't forgotten about her. I've still got another victory in store. It may not have happened yet, but I am true to My word. It's on the way."

Go around each day humming the refrain of that famous song and proclaiming the truth that God wants you to know. *I am unforgettable, in every way. God remembers me and that's how it will stay.*

Inside every one of us is the voice of God. Don't allow life to drown Him out. He is saying, "You are made in My image. You are valuable, you are significant, and you are important. I chose you because I love you."

Sometimes life tries to overpower that still, small voice. Life can get very loud. Unfair things happen. People talk negatively about us. Somebody walks out of our life. But what really matters is who you are and who God says you are. You may feel insignificant, but God sees you as valuable. He sees you as important. He calls you His masterpiece.

How you feel and what life has done to you doesn't change the value of your life in the eyes of God.

> *How you feel and what life has done to you doesn't change the value of your life in the eyes of God.*

If you take a new hundred-dollar bill and crumple it into a tiny ball, then put it in the washer and dryer a dozen times, it will look pretty worn. But it will still have the same value as it did when it was crisp and new. The value of that hundred-dollar bill is not affected by how it looks or how it feels. It still has the same buying power.

In the same way, it doesn't matter if life has put some wrinkles on you or put you through the wringer a couple dozen times. You may feel bruised and battered or fatigued to the point of breaking, but God's truth about you is that you have value and importance.

God is drawing you near. His eyes are on you. Press closer when He meets you at the well. Don't allow anyone to keep you bent over with their words or allow your circumstances to draw your gaze to the ground. No matter how difficult it is, keep looking up. You have all the power and authority to stand up straight, because Jesus has already called you forward and set you free.

EXCEPTIONAL THOUGHTS

+ No matter how big the world is, or how far away I feel from God, I will remember God knows everything about me, and He is always drawing me near to Him. He is not far away. He is up close and personal with me. He has closed any distance between us through Christ Jesus, and He is as close as the very breath I breathe.

+ Even in my worst times, God is drawing me close. He meets me wherever I am and offers me the living water of salvation. I will drink and He will heal my broken heart and fill my thirsty soul.

+ I will not allow the conditions of my life to keep me from my position of faith. I am a Child of the Promise, and God is calling me forward. I will stand up straight and take my position in this promise. Whom the Son sets free is free indeed.

+ I may have been through some setbacks and have a few wrinkles from life. But my value hasn't changed in the eyes of God. My life matters and I am important to God.

+ I am unforgettable to God. My name is written on the palms of His hands. I am the apple of His eye, His masterpiece. He has not forgotten about my dreams and goals. I believe it's just a matter of time before I reap my harvest.

CHAPTER 14

Connect to the Source

One of the best ways to enter into every day empowered, inspired, and intentional is to begin each day by spending time with God. It's so easy in the morning to pick up our phones and begin to look at our text messages and our emails, and to check out what's happening on social media. But in that small action, we are filling ourselves with the wrong things right from the start. And then time has gotten away from us and we have to rush to begin our day. Before we check in with the world, we should check in with God. We should fuel ourselves with His Word, His promises, and His proclamations, and then we'll enter each day with more power. He is our source. He knows what we need. If we are going to be our best and live exceptional, we need to get in a habit of spending time with God every day.

Ephesians 3 says, "I pray that out of his glorious riches he may strengthen you with power through his Spirit in your inner being, so that Christ may dwell in your hearts" (vv. 16–17). God wants to strengthen you "in your inner being." We have to focus not on the outer, but on the inner. Just like our physical body gets refreshed and reenergized when we sleep at night, we need to take time to strengthen and fuel our inner man. We can spend so much time getting our outer self ready for the day that we forget to get our inner self prepared for each day. And then we wonder why we're stressed out, struggling, and not able to make good decisions and overcome bad habits. It's because we're not taking time to keep our inner self strong.

Strengthen Your Core

Not long ago, I hurt my shoulder so badly that I couldn't lift my arm. It was incredibly painful, but I just muddled through and prayed that it would improve with rest. Then, about five days later, I woke up in the morning and could hardly stand up straight. Every time I tried to straighten my spine, I experienced intense pain in the lower part of my back. I couldn't imagine what I had done. Now, it takes a lot for me to go to the doctor but this pain was intense. I knew it was time to go in and get myself checked out. The doctor took X-rays and even did an MRI but couldn't find anything wrong with me. He told me I must have had some inflammation, but I had no torn muscles, no bulging disks, so he sent me to a physical therapist.

The physical therapist had me do a series of movements, simple things that we all do every day. He had me reach up with my arms extended as if I was reaching for something; he had me bend over to pick something up from the ground. He had me walk forward, then backward. After observing all my movements, he said, "Victoria, your core is weak. And your core is what helps you move your extremities without hurting yourself. Your core keeps you balanced and in alignment. You need to build up your inner core muscles and they will give you the support you need and help your body move without injury. If you don't start working on your core muscles, these injuries could become more frequent with time."

I walked out of there with a number of exercises to do every day to strengthen my core.

Your inner man is the core of who you are. And in much the same way as we need a strong core to be able to safely move our bodies, when we have a strong inner man, it engages the rest of our life and helps our life become easier. In fact, some of the hurts that we suffer come because we're not engaging our spiritual core. We can't allow our fickle feelings and emotions to run our lives. God wants you to be strong and have self-control so you can rise higher and go farther. A strong command center will cause you to walk in a posture of faith, confidence, and self-discipline.

Our inner man is our identity; it controls how we respond to life, and it shapes our attitudes and thoughts. When we have a strong inner man, it affects our entire life and helps us make good decisions. A strong core helps us hear from God, to get His direction for our life. When we pay attention to this core of who we are, we can move into each day with strength. You may say, "I'm so busy in the mornings. I have to get my kids to school. I am making

> *When we pay attention to this core of who we are, we can move into each day with strength.*

breakfast and getting lunches ready. It is so hectic. I don't have time to get quiet and strengthen my inner man." You are doing yourself a disservice. You have to take time to feed your inner man every day.

Joel's father used to say, "Some people feed their physical

bodies three hot meals a day, but they feed their spirit one cold snack a week." Every day you need to feed your inner man. Think about what you are nourishing yourself with. Reading the Scriptures is nourishing your inner man with spiritual food. Being quiet and thanking God for His goodness is spiritual food. Declaring God's promises over your life feeds the core of who you are. This is how you stir up your faith each and every morning, by feeding your inner man with the food that it craves. Then you can go out and get your kids ready, pack lunches, and you aren't running on empty; you are fueled with faith.

Don't go through your day feeling discouraged when you can start your day off right by thanking God for His blessings and preparing your mind to be productive. Every day get up and thank God for your health, your relationships, your family, and your job. By starting your day this way, your inner man is being nourished. When you align yourself with God, your outlook will become brighter and your attitude more positive. You will have more strength to turn an ordinary day into an exceptional one.

There have been many mornings I've gotten up and felt like I was dragging. I had no joy, no enthusiasm, thinking, *This day is going to be a struggle. I have so much to do.* I've learned when that happens, I don't have to just give in and go through the day lacking enthusiasm. I know more than ever I have to get to my quiet place and get my inner man fed and my faith stirred.

You may have a very busy schedule. There is always so much to do. Especially parents with young children. If you're not careful, you'll take care of everyone but yourself. You must make it a priority to keep yourself strong on the inside. If we are run down, physically and mentally, the smallest things can bother us and make us irritable. When that happens, it means we are out of balance and it's time to get quiet and refreshed and refuel the inner man.

The apostle Paul says, "Be strong in the Lord...empowered through your union with Him" (Eph. 6:10 AMPC). The Amplified Bible version of Jeremiah 29:13 says to require God "as a vital necessity." That means we can't have the attitude, "If I have time, I'll try to do this." We're not going to live exceptional that way. We're not going to be our best if we're not making God a vital part of our life. Think about that word *vital*. That means you can't live without it. You need it. Your life requires it.

Toward the end of Joel's father's life, he was on dialysis. He had to go three times a week. Not once did he ever say, "You know what? I don't feel like going today. I think I'll just stay home," or "I have a lot to do at the office; maybe I'll do it next time." That was never an option. Why? It was vital to his life. It didn't matter how he felt. It didn't matter what came up. His life depended on it.

That's the way we need to look at spending time with God. You have to set aside time with God as a vital part of your life.

> *You have to set aside time with God as a vital part of your life.*

What makes a good marriage? Spending time together. It's like my relationship with Joel. I've never once said, "Well, I better go talk to Joel today. I have to pay my dues. I did marry him." I delight in spending time with Joel. It strengthens our relationship and brings us closer together. That's how we should feel about our relationship with God. Not "I have to get up this morning and spend time with God. What a burden. Let me hurry and get it over with." No, God is waiting for us to draw near to Him, to call out to Him each day. Scripture says to call out to God and He will show

> *God wants to give you His strength for the day, mercy for your mistakes, and wisdom for your decisions.*

you great and mighty things. God wants to give you His strength for the day, mercy for your mistakes, and wisdom for your decisions. The reason some people are all stressed out, don't know what to do, and can't find peace and joy is because they never get in God's presence. There's stress during the day, kids that need attention, challenges at the office, and traffic on the freeway. All these things take strength from your inner man. If you are only feeding your spirit once or twice a week, that's not enough to stay strong. You have to get into God's presence on a daily basis if you're really going to be empowered.

There will always be something trying to pull you away from this commitment. But don't let the distractions win. You have to be determined. The enemy doesn't want you to spend time with God. You may have to turn the phone off. You may have to set the alarm thirty minutes earlier. You may have to reorganize some things to make spending time with God a priority. But it is always worth it.

Jesus said, "I am the bread of life. I am the living water. If you drink of Me you'll never thirst again." Are you drinking from the living water? That's God's Word, that's praise, that's thanksgiving. Even during the day when things come against us, it's stressful, and you have opportunities to get upset. Take a five-minute break to gather your thoughts and reach out to God. You can pray in your heart, "God, I need Your help. Thank You for Your peace. I'm asking for Your strength." When you do that, you just took a drink. You bring God's presence into your life. You strengthened your inner man. The Bible says that when our spirit connects with God's Spirit, something incredible happens—we are ignited with the power of

Almighty God. The strongest part of you is not your physical body or your emotional realm. The strongest part of you, the eternal part of you, is your spirit, your inner man, the core of who you are. When you connect the strongest part of you with the strongest Force in the universe, there's a powerful transformation that takes place. When you make God a priority and you take time to stay connected to Him, you will be empowered to overcome challenges, and He will give you His favor and direct your path even in the difficulties of life.

Switch on the Power

A friend of mine had just completed the renovation of her new house and she couldn't wait to have me over to give me a tour. They had completely gutted the house down to the studs. They rewired all the electrical. As we pulled into her driveway, she said, "You won't believe it, Victoria. It's like a brand-new house." As we walked in, she flipped the switch to turn on the lights but nothing happened. We walked a little farther into the dark house and she tried another switch but still no lights. It was warm in the house, so we realized the air-conditioning was not working either. This beautiful, newly wired house had no power.

My friend called her contractor and asked him why nothing was working. He told her that while they do their work, they shut off the power source. She needed to find the breaker box and flip the main switch. After getting directions to the box, she found the power switch, flipped it on, and there it was. The lights came on, the air conditioner began to hum, and that's when the tour began.

We can live our lives in much the same way without even realizing it. We don't know why things aren't working. We can't seem to find our way. It seems dark and we feel like everything is a struggle. It's not that we are faulty in any way; we just haven't turned on the power in our lives. Ephesians 3 says: To him who is able to do immeasurably more than all we can ask, think, or imagine, according to the *power* that is at work within us (see v. 20). It doesn't say according to how much power God has. It doesn't say anything about God's ability.

> *You are fully wired today; you just need to turn on the power by turning to God and asking Him to be your source.*

It is saying according to the *power that is working in us*. My friend's house had enough power for every need in the house. They could run the air-conditioning, turn on the lights, run all their electronics, and use the washer and the dryer all at the same time. The wiring was there to fill the house with power. It just needed to be turned on at the source.

You are fully wired today; you just need to turn on the power by turning to God and asking Him to be your source. He wants to give you power to resist temptation, to walk in integrity, and to give you His peace and joy. You can stand firm against the challenges and disappointments that try to weaken you. You have the ability to be a good parent, raise strong families, have successful careers, and be a blessing everywhere you go. But it all starts by plugging into the source of power.

We would never think about leaving our house without our cell phones charged up. And even then we take our charger or a charging pack so we won't lose power. Why would we think about running our life without being connected to the source of all *power*, Jesus?

By making this a priority in your life, you will be transformed.

You will feel empowered, you will feel inspired, and you will go forth in your life strengthened for whatever may come.

Build Up Reserves

I heard the other day about a church that had challenged its congregants to memorize a Bible verse for every letter of the alphabet. The pastor thought it would be a fun way for children to begin to learn the Word of God and store it in their hearts.

One young family at first tuned out, because their child was only three and a half. But the minister encouraged everyone to take part in the challenge, sharing that young children can often surprise us with how much they can remember. So this young father began to work with his son to memorize a verse per week. And sure enough, his son loved the challenge and surprised his father with his ability to memorize one verse after another. Finally after six months, this little boy had learned them all. His dad, being a proud father, took a video and posted it for some of his friends. Well, that video took off. No one could believe this little four-year-old child could recite all these verses by heart.[6]

That young father did a service for his child. He was storing in his heart the truth of God. And even though a four-year-old can't grasp all the meaning in those verses, there will come a day when he will understand those words, and they will come to him in moments of need. The Word of God is like seeds planted in your heart. They will come to fruition in time and strengthen you when the world seems to crumble around you.

> *The Word of God is like seeds planted in your heart.*

I heard about a young pastor who faced the unimaginable. His young son died in his sleep, with no explanation. He was no longer an infant; this wasn't a case of SIDS. This was just a tragedy with no scientific cause, a gaping question mark in this pastor's life.

As he stood in the emergency room, holding his son's lifeless body, he dug deep into his heart for the Word and promises of God. He proclaimed to the nursing staff and anyone who would listen: "If I did not have faith, this would be the worst moment of my life. If Jesus didn't die for my son, for all of us, I would not be able to keep going. But I know my son is in heaven more alive than ever and I will see him again."

He held fast to his faith and anchored himself to the God of all hope. He knew that the truth of God's Word was stronger than anything that tried to bring him down. That didn't mean he didn't grieve and that his heart wasn't broken, but he found his strength to move forward in God's Word.[7]

When you spend time with God and nurture that relationship, it strengthens your faith, and His grace can help you get through the unimaginable. You are powered up, not just for the daily struggles, but also for the big challenges in life. When you read the Word of God, you may not understand everything you read. You may think, *I'm wasting my time. I could be doing something else.* Realize that you are planting a seed of truth. In your time of need, God will make sure it comes alive, that it will nourish you and keep you strong. Joel's father always

> *When you spend time with God and nurture that relationship, it strengthens your faith, and His grace can help you get through the unimaginable.*

taught us, "Put the Word of God in you when you don't need it and it will come out of you when you do."

What I'm asking you to do is not difficult, but it's one of the most important habits you can ever form. If you don't have a regular quiet time, make a decision to start. Don't think it's not doing anything. It's not only keeping your inner man fed, but it is keeping you powered up and setting the tone for the day. God wants to fill you with the dunamis power of Christ. The Greek word *dunamis* is used over a hundred times in the New Testament. It refers to the strength, ability, and power of God. When you connect to God through Jesus, which is the source of power, God will give you His ability beyond what you can ask, think, or imagine.

Learn to get filled up before you go out. Make it a priority. Spending time with God is vital so you can be empowered. For some of you, this may be the only thing that's holding you back. You're talented, you're dedicated, you love God, but you're not being empowered each day. Your inner man is not being refueled and refreshed. Why don't you make these changes? Get up each morning and connect to the power source by spending time with God. Draw strength from Him. Receive His wisdom; receive His peace and receive His power. Then you'll be able to go out and fight the good fight of faith. I know if you'll do this, you'll come up higher and higher. God will pour out His blessings and favor and you'll live the exceptional life He has in store for you.

EXCEPTIONAL THOUGHTS

✦ I will enter into each day empowered, inspired, and intentional by spending time with God. I won't get so busy with all the other areas of my life that I neglect my inner man. I will strengthen the core of who I am by putting God's Word in my heart and mind.

✦ I will declare God's promises over my life, feeding my inner man and preparing my mind to be productive.

✦ I have the power of God inside of me to resist temptation, to walk in integrity, and to have the peace and joy to lead and guide me along the paths of success.

✦ I will nurture my relationship with God and it will strengthen my faith, and He will give me the grace to get through the challenges of life.

✦ I am strong in the Lord and empowered through my union with Him. I will set aside time with God as a vital part of my life.

ACKNOWLEDGMENTS

I have discovered that most accomplishments borne through discipline, patience, and diligent effort are the most satisfying of all. Whether it be a lifetime of faith, the rearing of children, or writing a book, when we put everything we have into something and give it our best effort, we can step back from the finished product and say, "I'm proud of what I've done." The effort we put into everything we do in our life should be as rewarding as the result.

I was blessed to work with so many excellent people; it has been a joyful endeavor and a rewarding one. To all of them I owe my appreciation and gratitude.

First, I want to thank everyone at FaithWords/Hachette who brought their exceptional talents to this book, especially Rolf Zettersten, Patsy Jones, and Hannah Phillips.

I also want to thank my literary agents Jan Miller and Shannon Marven and the exceptional team at Dupree Miller for their friendship and loyalty and for thinking as big as we do.

When we stay in faith, God always brings the right people across our paths at the appropriate time and season. I would like to thank Cindy DiTiberio and Lance Wubbels for their exceptional insight on this journey.

It is always a pleasure to work with those who strive for excellence. I extend a special thank-you to Joe Gonzales for the cover design and Joseph West for the photography. Thank you to the Champions Network pastors for their friendship through the years, and Phil Munsey, a pastor's pastor who is always a voice of encouragement. Special thank you to my dear friend Roxanne Worsham, who is truly one of the most faithful and dependable people I know.

My warmest gratitude I extend to the Lakewood Church family and our extraordinary staff. Together we are accomplishing the most important mission of all: sharing the love and hope of our Savior with the world.

I am grateful to have grown up in the family God gave to me. My mother, Georgine, and my father, Donald, love me dearly and instilled in me—from the beginning—a sense of purpose and destiny. They took me to church and modeled for me the faith and values that I still possess today. Because of them, I have passed these blessings to my children, as they will do for theirs.

My brother, Donald Jr., is a guiding light in our ministry and in my life. I am grateful for his wisdom, his steadfast support, and his belief in me. I am blessed to have a brother like him.

I cannot sufficiently convey the love and gratitude in my heart for how wonderful and extraordinary my husband and children have made my life. My husband, Joel, is the love I always hoped for. He is my best friend, and the person who encourages me the most to achieve all that God has planned for me. The day I met Joel was a dream come true and I cherish the love he has always shown me. When God gave to me my children, Jonathan and Alexandra, He placed in my life the very sunshine that rises each day. They fill my life with joy, laughter, and love, and they make me proud to be their mom every day.

Finally, and most important, I want to give my eternal gratitude and praise to my Lord and Savior, Jesus Christ. I dedicate this work to Him, because words are only words until He breathes His life into them.

NOTES

Chapter 3: Set Your Eyes on the Promises

1. Lang Chen et al., "Positive Attitude Toward Math Supports Early Academic Success: Behavioral Evidence and Neurocognitive Mechanisms," *Psychological Science* 29, no. 3 (March 2018): 390–402, https://journals.sagepub.com/doi/10.1177/0956797617735528.

Chapter 9: Better Together

2. Brooke Pryor, "Kissing Bandit: Why Tom Herman Kisses Each Player Before a Game," NewsOK, October 12, 2017, https://newsok.com/article/5567853/kissing-bandit-why-tom-herman-kisses-each-player-before-a-game; Marc Tracy, "Houston's Coach Pecks Away at Football's Macho Culture, a Kiss at a Time," *New York Times*, October 15, 2016, https://www.nytimes.com/2016/10/16/sports/ncaafootball/houston-cougars-tom-herman-kiss-macho-culture.html; "Herman Supports Kissing Players on the Cheek," ESPN, http://www.espn.com/video/clip?id=20112376.

Chapter 10: Become a Blessing

3. Ahmar Mubeen, "2 Year Old Girl Watching a Movie and Crying Because the Dinosaur Fell and Lost His Mom," YouTube, video, 1:36, November 12, 2017, https://www.youtube.com/watch?v=fk0uFIZHEqs.
4. Billy Hallowell, "Selfless Commuter Gives Shoes off His Own Feet to Older Homeless Man Struggling in FREEZING Chicago Winter," FaithWire, January 15, 2018, https://www.faithwire.com/2018/01/15/selfless-commuter-takes-expensive-shoes-off-his-own-feet-to-give-to-bloodied-homeless-man-wearing-tattered-shoes-in-the-cold-of-winter/.

5. Maria Henson, "Walking with the Hope," *Wake Forest Magazine*, Fall 2018, https://magazine.wfu.edu/2018/10/03/walking-with-the-hope/.

Chapter 14: Connect to the Source

6. Jonathan Peterson, "4-Year-Old Recites ABCs Using Bible Verses," Bible Gateway, January 23, 2017, https://www.biblegateway.com/blog/2017/01/4-year-old-recites-abcs-using-bible-verses/.

7. Cameron Cole, *Therefore I Have Hope* (Wheaton, IL: Crossway, 2018).

ABOUT THE AUTHOR

Credit: Joseph West

VICTORIA OSTEEN is the co-pastor of Lakewood Church, the *New York Times* bestselling author of *Love Your Life*, and the host of a national weekly radio program, *Victoria Osteen Live*, on Sirius XM's Joel Osteen Radio. She is an integral part of each service at Lakewood as well as the "Night of Hope" events across the United States and abroad. She lives with her family in Houston, Texas.

Stay connected, be blessed.

Get more from
Joel & Victoria Osteen

It's time to step into the life of victory and favor that God has planned for you! Featuring new messages from Joel & Victoria Osteen, their free daily devotional and inspiring articles, hope is always at your fingertips with the free Joel Osteen app and online at JoelOsteen.com.

Get the app and visit us today at JoelOsteen.com.

JOEL OSTEEN
MINISTRIES

CONNECT WITH US

We Want to Hear from You!

Each week, we close our international television broadcast by giving the audience an opportunity to make Jesus the Lord of their lives. I'd like to extend that same opportunity to you.

Are you at peace with God? A void exists in every person's heart that only God can fill. I'm not talking about joining a church or finding religion. I'm talking about finding life and peace and happiness. Would you pray with me today? Just say, "Lord Jesus, I repent of my sins. I ask You to come into my heart. I make You my Lord and Savior."

If you prayed that simple prayer, I believe you have been "born again." I encourage you to attend a good Bible-based church and keep God in first place in your life. For free information on how you can grow stronger in your spiritual life, please feel free to contact us.

Joel and I love you, and we'll be praying for you. We're believing for God's best for you, that you will see your dreams come to pass. We'd love to hear from you!

To contact us, write to:

Joel and Victoria Osteen
P.O. Box 4600
Houston, TX 77210

Or you can reach us online at www.joelosteen.com.